MORE
TALES *from the*
DUGOUT

MORE
TALES *from the*
DUGOUT

More of the Greatest
True Baseball Stories
of All Time

Mike Shannon

McGraw·Hill

New York   Chicago   San Francisco   Lisbon   London   Madrid   Mexico City
Milan   New Delhi   San Juan   Seoul   Singapore   Sydney   Toronto

The *McGraw·Hill* Companies

Library of Congress Cataloging-in-Publication Data

Shannon, Mike.
   More tales from the dugout : More of the greatest true baseball stories of all
time / Mike Shannon.—1st ed.
      p.   cm.
   ISBN 0-07-141789-3
   1. Baseball—United States—Anecdotes.   I. Title.

GV873.S415   2004
796.357—dc22   2003018948

1 2 3 4 5 6 7 8 9 0   AGM/AGM   3 2 1 0 9 8 7 6 5 4

ISBN 0-07-141789-3

Interior illustrations by Don Pollard

McGraw-Hill books are available at special quantity discounts to use as premiums and
sales promotions, or for use in corporate training programs. For more information, please
write to the Director of Special Sales, Professional Publishing, McGraw-Hill, Two Penn
Plaza, New York, NY 10121-2298. Or contact your local bookstore.

This book is printed on acid-free paper.

CONTENTS

PREFACE

"Hello, everybody! This is Mike Shannon, coming to you once again from The Great American Ballpark on the banks of the beautiful Ohio River for today's game between the Cincinnati Reds and the . . ."

Excuse me, friends, I was just doing a little daydreaming there. You see, both members of the Reds' radio broadcasting team, Joe Nuxhall and Marty Brennaman, one of the longest-working and most beloved duos in major league broadcasting history, are going to be retiring soon, and the Reds are going to, you know, have to find replacements for them. I've never told anyone this before, but my secret ambition is to become a baseball radio broadcaster. And I figure, hey, why not start at the top?

I'm just kidding, of course. Not about wanting to become a broadcaster, but about expecting to start at the top. I know full well how ridiculous even the thought of such a thing is, and I would be punch-drunk happy to start at the bottom—although by the bottom I'm not talking about the local neighborhood Pee Wee finals. The low minor leagues, that's what I'm talking about. And, believe it or not, I actually already have some experience under my belt in that arena.

It came when I was working on a different book, which is soon going to be turned into a movie, with Clint Eastwood starring as yours truly, called *Everything Happens in Chillicothe: A Summer in the Frontier League with Max McLeary, the One-Eyed Umpire*. The book is an account of the 2000 season, which I spent following Mr. McLeary in his travels around an independent professional baseball circuit, with teams located throughout the Midwest. During the course of that summer I became fast friends with Gary Kitchel, the play-by-play man of the Richmond (Indiana) Roosters. While Gary, who does a wonderful job for the Roosters, doesn't need any help, he's always inviting other people to join him on the air for a few innings as unofficial "color commentators"—folks such as the *Richmond Palladium-Item* beat man, the baseball coach at nearby Earlham College, one of the McBride Stadium beer vendors, the famous Chicken, me.

My initial stint on the air with Gary was ear-opening and educational, at least for me. One of the first things I learned is that as a color commentator you have to get to the point quickly. Trying to describe the experience in *Everything Happens in Chillicothe*, I wrote, "If you want to know what being rushed feels like, imagine being in the midst of an explanation you know all of a sudden is too long while a pitcher is coming to the plate."

Gary and I, as well as Gary's listeners, survived my color commentating debut, and I like to think that I got better as the season went on. If I were to get a chance at my own play-by-play job, I know I wouldn't start off being as good as Kitch or Matt Andrews, the kid who went from the Chillicothe Paints straight to the Triple-A Louisville Bats as their second man in the booth; but I think I could do the job. As John Fogarty says in "Centerfield," "Put me in, Coach."

Getting back to reality—yes, we have to—I'm not coming to you from the broadcast booth of The Great American Ballpark or even from The Dugout. No, I'm coming to you from The Basement—of my home, where my writing office is located. That's not as incongruous as it may seem to be, though, considering the fact that there is nothing to be found in a dugout, besides tobacco-juice spit on the floor, that is not also to be found in my basement office, which, on the other hand, contains a zillion baseball items you won't ever see in a dugout. In fact, my office screams BASEBALL! at you so loudly and clearly that my wife, Derms, won't even set foot in the place. My office is so crammed with baseball books, magazines, newspapers, pictures, cards, more books, figurines, bats and balls, and even more books that it gives her a headache just to see it all. Maybe it's the thought of having to organize all that crap or dust it that gets her; I don't know.

The point is that while the stories in this book were polished for you in The Basement, I did originally find them in the dugouts of America, both literally and figuratively; meaning that I went out and personally talked to the actual storytellers behind the tales in the book. Some of these people I found at the ballpark, and some of them I found away from it. Some I even found in their own basement offices. At any rate, I want to express my gratitude to all of them; the ones named in the text itself, as well as others I will acknowledge here in a few moments.

Contrary to what some people think, getting material for a book like this is hard work, and you strike out far more often than you hit a home run. First of all, some of the people willing to talk just don't have good stories. You never know whether they do or not until you talk to them. Others have good stories, but they are the kind of tales that fall under the category of "Adult Material" and are thus not suitable for publication in *More Tales from the Dugout*, which I am proud to believe can be read by baseball-loving youngsters without objection from their parents. Someday I may collect all of this X-rated baseball material and publish it in a book entitled *The Little Black Book of Baseball*; if I do, I'll leave out all the real names, including my own, to protect the guilty. You'll know it's me if the cover says the book was written by "Anonymous."

And then, although it doesn't happen often, sometimes you get rejected out of hand. The most memorable instance of this happened to me in Cooperstown, New York, of all places. During one Hall of Fame induction weekend, an event I have been covering for various publications since 1986, I went into one of the baseball memorabilia stores that have proliferated in Cooperstown like illegal immigrants in California, seeking some material for one of my books. Inside the store—in the basement, as a matter of fact—sat two Hall of Fame players who were signing autographs for a fee: former Red Sox second baseman Bobby Doerr and a pitcher who'd only recently been inducted into baseball's most exclusive fraternity. The autograph business was pretty slow, so it was easy for me to walk right up to the table they were sitting at and start talking. When I introduced myself to the pitcher and explained what I was after, he snarled contemptuously, "How much money you got!"

Without responding to this rebuff, I turned and tried Mr. Doerr, who acted, completely in character, like a gentleman. "This isn't the best time to talk right now," he said, "but I'll give you my home phone number, and if you call me next week, we can talk then and I'm sure I can tell you something for your book."

As I walked out of the room, after thanking Doerr, I heard somebody behind me call out, "Captain! Hey, Captain!"

I was still a little embarrassed as well as unsure whether I was the one being addressed, and so I didn't stop and turn around. Later, I realized it was the Hall of Fame newcomer who'd tried to get my attention after he'd had a chance to think about what had just happened. I imagine his thinking went something like this: "I was pretty rude to this guy, and then Doerr goes and gives him his home phone number—and the guy is a writer. What if he writes about how I acted? I'm not going to look so good compared with Doerr."

Fortunately, I don't have many "what's it like to be a writer?" stories like that one. Far more typical are the encounters I've had with people like Bill McKeon and Kent Tekulve.

Bill McKeon is the brother of cigar-chomping Jack McKeon, who has managed five different major league ballclubs. When he was in charge of the San Diego Padres, Bill's brother made so many deals he became known as "Trader Jack." In 1989 he even traded his son-in-law, catcher Greg Booker, to the Minnesota Twins. Like his more famous brother, Bill has been in professional baseball for most of his life. There wasn't much in it for him, but Bill graciously consented to talk to me, and he went nonstop for an entire afternoon before a game at Bosse Field in Evansville, Indiana. I knew Bill was going to be good when he said, "As I always tell people, 'Behind every story, there's another story.'" One of these stories-behind-the-story was about the time Bill accidentally discovered that he and his brother had been mispronouncing their own surname all their lives. Bill went into a hotel where Jack was staying and asked the girl at the front desk, a pretty Irish lass (is there any other kind?), for the room number of his brother. The girl told him no such person was registered at the hotel. Bill assured her that his brother was there. He even pronounced the name extra carefully for her: "Mc-Kee-on." She assured him that nobody with such a name was at the hotel. In exasperation Bill finally spelled out the last name for the girl, who immediately said, "Oh, you mean 'McQune.' Why, yes, Jack McQune is in room so-and-so."

While Bill McKeon, I mean "McQune," was a rich vein of material, I might have mined even more of it had I not given Bill the wrong impression initially. In trying to give him some examples of topics he might discuss, I mentioned "fights." Two hours later it finally dawned on me that Bill thought that baseball fight stories were all that I was looking for. Before we changed the subject, he told me some doozies.

One of these stories involved a young Roger Maris when he played for Fargo in the old Class C Northern League in the early 1950s. McKeon, a blabbermouth even back then, was catching for Eau Claire and talking away as usual, which highly irritated Maris for some reason. When McKeon came to bat, Maris, who was not in the lineup that day, hollered from the Fargo dugout, "Hey, Catfish, why don't you go sit down right now and save our pitcher the trouble of having to strike your ass out!" (Bill explained that Maris's Catfish crack was a reference to his having a big mouth.)

After grounding out to second, Bill turned and ran into the Fargo dugout to accost Maris. He didn't get anywhere near Maris though because two huge second-string catchers grabbed him and lifted him off the ground. "You got a problem, buddy?" they asked.

"No, no—no problem," said Bill, wondering the whole time as he was suspended in the air, Where are my teammates!

After the pair of brutes threw McKeon face-first into the dirt in front of the Fargo dugout, Bill returned sheepishly to the Eau Claire dugout. "Where were you guys? Why didn't you back me up," he demanded to know.

"We love you, Bill, but we're not messing with those big guys," his teammates said.

Another fight story centered around Earl Weaver, when Weaver had just begun his managerial career with Fitzgerald of the Class D Georgia-Florida League. This was in the days when player-managers were common in the minor leagues, and both Weaver and McKeon were playing managers. McKeon had a good bench jockey on his Waycross team who got under Weaver's skin and went a little too far when he said something insulting about Earl's mother. Enraged, Weaver charged across the diamond, leaped feet first into the Waycross dugout, and planted the spikes of both shoes into the thighs of the first person in his path, a Wisconsin farmer who happened to be the biggest, strongest, and meanest player on McKeon's team. According to McKeon, this giant of a farmer-ballplayer grabbed Weaver; punched him in the face—boom, boom, boom—and then lifted him up so powerfully that Weaver's head literally broke through the top of the dugout, rendering Fitzgerald's fearless leader unconscious. In the meantime, McKeon himself beat the stuffing out of the Fitzgerald shortstop who tried to come to Weaver's aid. Although nobody got thrown out of the game by the umpires, Fitzgerald lost two players (Weaver and the shortstop) who were taken to the hospital.

Later in the game Fitzgerald retaliated when one of their pitchers broke two of McKeon's ribs with a pitched ball. The broken ribs hurt so bad that McKeon had to sit on first base for a while in order to catch his breath. As play resumed, Bill called for the hit and run and took off with the pitch. The batter hit a grounder to second, and as the shortstop came across the bag to take the throw, the sliding McKeon intentionally sliced him across the thigh with his spikes. When the shortstop tried to hit McKeon in the face with the ball, the brawl was on. "The Fitzgerald fans nearly rioted," said Bill. "They were trying to hit us with rakes and shovels, and we needed a police escort to get out of the ballpark alive."

Geez, Bill, I thought, for such a nice guy, you sure could be a mean bastard.

Kent Tekulve, who played during a more genteel era than McKeon, was also very generous with his time and memories. In fact, I was so delighted with the tales he told me that I forgot to get from him the details of the one story I came prepared to ask him about. A second-hand version of it will still give you a good idea about the type of person Tekulve is. To commemorate the last baseball game ever played at Pittsburgh's Three Rivers Stadium, on October 1, 2000, the Pirates brought back a number of players from the team's past, who were introduced on the field at the conclusion of the game between the Pirates and the Chicago Cubs. The last player scheduled to be introduced was Tekulve, who was supposed to deliver the last pitch ever thrown in the ballpark in honor of the many times he had closed out Pirates victories at Three Rivers. Tekulve followed the script by making his appearance to the sound of "Rubber Band Man," the song the Pirates had always played as his introductory music when he was coming in from the bullpen; but he didn't, as expected, close out the Three Rivers era in Pirates history. Instead, he called over his old friend and teammate, the ailing Willie Stargell, and insisted that "Pops" have the honor of throwing to catcher Jason Kendall the ceremonial final pitch. The gesture touched everyone who saw it and illustrated better than any words could have the bond of brotherhood that made the 1979 Pirates a loving baseball family.

The stories in this book are meant to entertain above all else, but I would like to think that more than a few of them are also inspirational to some degree or another. Whether you want to be a better ballplayer, a better friend, or a better person, there are good examples in this book to follow. I certainly have been inspired to follow my dream, the one I started off this Preface talking about, by the fortunes, if not quite the methods, of a young minor league broadcaster I met during the course of my research. Much to my astonishment, this young fellow told me that he had never broadcast a sporting event of any kind before landing his present job. He was hired on the basis of a good interview and a self-made audition tape of himself pretending to broadcast a college baseball game played by his alma mater during the spring of his senior year. The young man wasn't even a communications major in college. Nevertheless, the minor league team, which is very happy with his performance, selected him from a field of more than fifty seemingly better qualified candidates. Someday, he'll be in a position to spill the beans and have quite a laugh over his chutzpa; but for now his identity, if not his story, must remain a secret. As for me, while I have a dream that obviously is not a total fantasy, I won't be shattered if the dream is never realized. After all, being able to write this book and its predecessors has been a dream come true already.

As usual, the list of people I am indebted to for help with this book is long and includes: Cindi Andrews and John Erardi of the *Cincinnati Enquirer*; Todd Bell and Colin Lattimer of the Columbus Clippers; Carl Bouldin; Mike Caldwell; Steve Campbell of the *Albany Times-Union*; Jim Crowley; Roger and Wil Davidson of Davidson's Jewelry in Cooperstown, New York (Go Tigers!); Brad Del Barba; Matt Dixon and Eric Redlinger, sentries supreme of the Washington (Pennsylvania) Wild Things; Dr. Chris Hanners, DDS; Tim Harms and Blake Kirkman of the Indianapolis Indians; Jerry Hazelbaker; Wally Herbert; Jeff Idelson of the National Baseball Hall of Fame and Museum; Tom Jackson; Svend Jansen, Matt Andrews, and Jim Kelch of the Louisville Bats; Jeremy Kelly and Jim Smith of "Sports, etc."; Adam Knollman and Eric Minshall of the Florence Freedom; Dave Koch of the Cincinnati Red Stockings' vintage baseball team; Dr. Michael G. Leadbetter, M.D.; Bill Lee, commissioner of the Frontier League; Neil Luken; Hal McCoy; Bill McGill, managing editor of *Spitball: The Literary Baseball Magazine*; Max McLeary; Willis Monie and son of Willis Monie Used & Rare Books in Cooperstown, New York; Bryan Mullen of the *Florida Times-Union*; Brian and Becky Nielsen of Augur's Books in Cooperstown, New York; Bob Nightengale; Bob Pickford; Gaylen Pitts; Bobby Plapinger; Jeff Pohl of the Evansville Otters; David Rankin; Greg Rhodes; Mark and Jeannie Schraf; Mark Schmetzer of *Reds Report*; Charlie Vascellaro; Bob Walsh; and Josh Whetzel of the Rochester Red Wings.

I tell friends all the time "It's not easy to write a good book, but it is easier to write a good book than to find a publisher for one." Matthew Carnicelli of McGraw-Hill believed that it was time for another *Tales from the Dugout* book, and I am grateful to him for that. I also thank his assistant, Mandy Huber, for her cheerful assistance and guidance.

My large and loyal family continues to be the biggest blessing in my life, and words cannot convey the love and gratitude

I feel toward them all, especially my parents, John and Willie Shannon. My sisters, Laura and Susie, and my brothers, John and Tim, are my biggest fans, as I am theirs. They all have their own families, made up of wonderful people who are always good to me, and I thank them too: Jeff and Andrew Smiley (the genius of our family); Lyle and Evan Klemmt; Janice (nee Veraneau), John, Rachel, and Laura Shannon; and Carla (nee Gowan), Riley, and Claire Shannon.

Special thanks must go to my children: Meg, Casey, Mickey, Babe, and Nolan Ryan; to Meg's husband, Vince Patterson, and to their children, Maeve and McKenna; and to my wife and Tennessee honey, Kathy, aka Derms. Because of you, The Basement is never a lonely place.

MORE
TALES *from the*
DUGOUT

RICHIE ASHBURN

Possessing one of the most recognizable voices in sports broadcasting, Harry Kalas has been calling the games of the Philadelphia Phillies since 1971. For many years Kalas's partner was Richie "Whitey" Ashburn, who went into broadcasting after completing his Hall of Fame career as a center fielder for the Phillies and New York Mets. To illustrate Ashburn's great sense of humor, Kalas tells the following story.

"Richie Ashburn was a joy to work with because he not only brought baseball expertise to the broadcasting booth but laughter as well," says Kalas.

"One thing that Whitey used to do—when it would be getting late in the evening, and we were getting hungry—he'd say, 'I wonder if the folks at Celebre's Pizza are listening to the broadcast?' And, of course, fifteen minutes later two delicious pizzas would be delivered to the press box.

"Well, after he did this for a while, the Phillies' brass called him in and said, 'Look, Richie, you can't be giving away free plugs during the broadcast to Celebre's Pizza—they're not one of our sponsors.'

"Now, we may not have been allowed to give away free advertising, but we were always allowed to mention people's birthdays and anniversaries, to offer our congratulations for things like that. So the next night, it got to be about that time in the game, and we were getting hungry as usual. So about the seventh inning, Richie said, 'Harry, I'd like to send out our warmest birthday greetings to the Celebre's twins—Plain and Pepperoni!' "

JOE AUSANIO

In the old days, rookies were often not welcomed onto a major league ballclub. For one thing, the arrival of a rookie usually meant the release of a veteran who was already the friend of the other players. For another, it was considered standard operating procedure to abuse rookies in order to test them.

Rookies these days still undergo some hazing, but, as the experiences of Joe Ausanio show, the harassment is generally good natured. Ausanio was a hard-throwing relief pitcher who made his major league debut in 1994 with the New York Yankees, after having languished for several years in the farm system of the Pittsburgh Pirates.

"The day they called me up was a whirlwind," says Joe. "I'm from Kingston, New York, so having heard about the Yankees all my life, it was an awesome thing just to walk into Yankee Stadium as a player for the first time. The next thing I know I'm in the Yankees' clubhouse, I'm getting fitted for a Yankees uniform, and I'm meeting all these great ballplayers who are now my teammates. We have a workout, and then before I can catch my breath we're on a bus to Newark Airport, because we're flying to Seattle to start a new series. It had been a long, exciting day for me, and I was worn out, so I thought I'd get some sleep on the plane—no way. Pitcher Bob Wickman kept waking me up, saying, 'Hey, rookie, no rookies sleeping on the plane.'

"I said, 'Ah, come on, Bob. Just let me sleep for a couple of hours.' Nope. So I got up and started playing cards with them. As luck would have it, I wiped them all out, and of course they didn't like that a whole lot either.

"When we got back to New York, we opened a series at home against the Boston Red Sox, and I was excited to see that former Red Sox outfielder Jim Rice was Boston's hitting instructor. I grabbed a couple of new baseballs and went over to ask him to autograph them. I told him that he had been my favorite player when I was a kid. He said, 'You liked me?' I guess he was surprised to hear me say that because he is kind of intimidating. He's a big strong guy, usually has a scowl on his face, and had a reputation for being surly with the media. I said, 'Yes, sir, I liked you, very much. You want to know your batting stats for 1979?' He laughed, signed the balls, and wished me luck. I was thrilled to get his autograph, but my teammates on the Yankees really ragged me about it as being a bush league thing to do—to ask the opposition for an autograph, and they fined me for it in kangaroo court. But I didn't care. I was glad I'd done it, because I didn't know if I'd ever get the chance to get Jim Rice's autograph again.

"My teammates screwed with me in some other, little ways, but really they were great to me. The other guys in the bullpen in particular, pitchers Steve Howe, Bob Wickman, and Xavier Hernandez, really took me under their wing. They were the best. And they wouldn't let me pay for anything. They never let me pay for a cab or pick up a lunch tab, even though I was earning more money than I ever had before in my life. It was always 'Put your money away, rook.' I guess my rookie money just wasn't any good to them. One day I finally pleaded with Xavier Hernandez to let me pay for breakfast. He said, 'Okay. Give me twenty dollars.'

"When I pulled out a twenty-dollar bill and handed it to him, he ripped it in half and gave the pieces back to me. He said, 'If you ever try to give me money again, I'm going to rip it in half again.'

"So I said, 'Okay. Don't worry. I'll never try to give you money again.'"

DOUG BAIR

Relief pitcher Doug Bair faced a long, tough road to get to the big time, but he never gave up and finally made his debut in the major leagues in 1976 with the Pittsburgh Pirates when he was twenty-seven years old. Although Bair never duplicated his best season, when he won 7 games, saved 28, and fashioned a sparkling 1.97 ERA for the Cincinnati Reds in 1978; he competed ferociously every spring for a job in baseball, and he wound up putting together a fifteen-year career with seven different major league clubs.

Bair truly loved to play the game, so much so that after he retired from professional baseball he played amateur ball for several summers in an over-thirty men's league in Cincinnati. Bair's approach to pitching in these amateur games was the same as it had been when he was a pro, and the players in the men's league hung the nickname "Rambo" on him.

Bill Loughery, one of the players in the Cincinnati men's league, tells a story that reveals this side of Bair's personality. "In the winter of 1991 my buddy Mel Kattelman got a call from Bair, who asked if he could work out with us at the batting cage," says Loughery. "Bair, who'd been released by Pittsburgh, wanted to get ready for spring training tryouts because he still wanted to pitch in the big leagues. Of course, Mel told him, sure, come on over.

"The next day Bair comes out to the batting cage, and Mel and I are thrilled to meet him. Bair asks if one of us can warm him up, so Mel grabs a catcher's mitt and Bair starts throwing to him. When Bair gets loose, he turns to me and asks if I want to hit. So I jump into the cage and step up to the plate. Bair throws me eight or nine pretty good fastballs, and I hit them okay, and then he says he's going to throw eight or nine curveballs. Once I see how the ball is breaking I hit some of them okay, too. Then Bair says he's going to throw some sliders. The first one comes in, it breaks pretty good, and I just look at it. And Bair gets all excited. 'Oh, my gosh!' he says. 'That's unhittable! That's a major league slider! That's a Rob Dibble slider!'

"Well, he throws me another good slider, and I just get a piece of it. Foul tip it. By now I know how it's going to break, so when he throws the third one, I'm able to meet it. I don't hit it hard. I just kind of lean out and stick the bat on the ball, and it flares off to the right side of the cage.

"The next pitch is a fastball, right at my head. He doesn't throw it as fast as he can, and I'm able to pull my head out of the way, but it's definitely a brush-back pitch. Mel and I can't believe it. We barely know the guy, and it's just a practice session. But none of that matters to Bair. He comes off the mound, walks halfway to the plate, and says, 'Billy, Billy—that part of the plate out there on the outside corner—that belongs to me.' "

MARY BARNEY

Professional baseball is still pretty much an all-male domain. And while it is no longer rare to find a female in a front-office position, it takes a special woman to earn a real place in the old boys' club that rules the game. Such a person is Mary Barney, a longtime employee of the Triple-A Louisville Bats and the team's current director of baseball operations.

Surprisingly enough, Barney did not acquire her love of baseball from either her father or her husband. She grew up in Chicago and developed an attachment to the Cubs pretty much by herself, thank you very much. "We were the first family on the block to own a television, and I never missed a Cubs game on WGN," says Barney. "People ask me how I came to love baseball, and I tell them that the only time I ever ironed was when the Cubs were on TV. They think I'm kidding, but I'm not." Okay, but it's a long way from being just another Cubs fan to achieving a high-level front-office position with a Triple-A franchise, and in making that leap Barney had help from her husband. But just a little.

Barney's husband was a big-shot advertising executive in Chicago. After he got transferred to Louisville, he picked up the Bats' predecessors, the Louisville Redbirds, as an account. With her kids in school, Barney decided she wanted to work outside the home, doing something she would love to do, so she set her sights on the Redbirds. Her husband's relationship with the team may have gotten her foot inside the door, but Mary herself had to convince A. Ray Smith, the team's crusty, eccentric owner, that she knew baseball. "When A. Ray interviewed me, he asked me what the number seven means," says Mary. "I told him, 'Mickey Mantle.' I knew he didn't mean the left fielder, which is number seven in scorekeeping, so he could see that I did know baseball. After the interview, A. Ray invited my husband and me to a big dinner the organization had to celebrate the signing of Ken Boyer as our manager, and he placed me at the table between Boyer and Lee Thomas, who was the Cardinals' farm director at the time—again as a 'Let's see if she knows baseball' test. I remember that Thomas was impressed when I said, 'Didn't you play for the Cubs and later in Japan toward the end of your career?' So I got the job."

The testing didn't stop there, but Mary showed she could handle the kidding and whatever else the guys wanted to dish out. "One day Tracy Woodson asked me to sew the strap back onto his jock, which had turned pink in the laundry, by the way. Mike Jorgensen, an ex–big leaguer who was working in the Cardinals' scouting department, called me on the phone and asked what I was doing. 'Sewing up Tracy Woodson's jock strap,' I said. He laughed and said, 'No, really, Mary. What are you up to?' I knew he was in on the joke, so I just played along and didn't get mad about it."

A lot of the ball club's players and young front-office interns started calling Barney "Mom" because she would do little things to take care of them and because they knew they could always come into her office to talk to her. When that same Tracy Woodson was knocked unconscious in a collision at first base in the last game of the season one year, it was Barney who stayed behind in an Indianapolis hospital to mother him. "To make sure that Tracy did not lapse into a coma, I had to wake him up every two hours," she says. "I stayed up all night with a book and a Diet Coke."

Barney's sense of humor and concern for others made her popular, but she moved right on up the ladder to her present position because she was dedicated, talented, and, most of all, trustworthy. "I proved that I could keep my mouth shut when it was necessary, to protect the integrity of trades, roster moves, and the like," she says, "and I slowly gained access into the 'inner sanctums.'"

Barney was finally recognized for her accomplishments and contributions to the game when she won the 2000 Professional Baseball Woman Executive of the Year Award, which is presented by the Rawlings Sporting Goods Company. "I think every woman in the game, if she knows of the award, aspires to win it," says Barney. When she learned that she was going to be presented with the award at the baseball winter meetings, she realized she would have to give an acceptance speech. "I was reminded of the Oscars and how boring I think the speeches are when the winners go on and on thanking everybody, but then I realized that you do have to thank a lot of people because you don't have your success by yourself. A lot of other people contribute to it. My husband, who is an advertising writer, said, 'Don't you want me to write your speech for you?'

"I said, 'No. I certainly do not.' I can't remember all that much about what I said besides thanking a lot of people, but I do remember the line I closed with. The winter meetings took place that year in the middle of the voting mess between George Bush and Al Gore, so I said: 'You may not know who the next president of the United States is, but you do know who the proudest woman in professional baseball is.'

"When I got back to our table, my husband said, 'Bravo! I couldn't have done any better.'"

JOHNNY BENCH

Blessed with great physical abilities—he could dunk a basketball and hold six baseballs in one hand—Johnny Bench is also smarter than the average bear. The valedictorian of his high school class, Bench has always displayed a good sense of humor, a sure sign of intelligence. In kidding good-naturedly about the size of his hometown of Binger, Oklahoma, Bench once said: "After I won the National League Rookie of the Year Award in 1968, Binger held a parade in my honor. There was nobody standing on the sidewalks when the parade went by because everybody in town was in the parade."

Another thing about Johnny Bench: during his major league career he was the consummate clutch player. Here are only two of the many examples of that ability to perform at his best when the pressure was on. In the fifth and deciding game of the 1972 National League playoffs between the Cincinnati Reds and the Pittsburgh Pirates, Bench lead off the bottom of the ninth inning with the Reds trailing by a run. Johnny's mother walked down to the railing by the dugout and pleaded with her son to hit a home run. The obedient Bench did just that, tying the game, which the Reds then went on to win. Eleven years later Bench was honored at Riverfront Stadium during the final month of his career. In front of an electrified sellout crowd, Bench was showered with going-away presents. Many friends and teammates delivered testimonials to his greatness, and then Bench himself addressed the crowd, concluding his short speech with the promise that "I am going to try like hell to play good for you tonight." In the first inning Houston Astros pitcher

Mike Madden walked Bench, drawing a chorus of boos from the crowd, but in the third inning Bench came to bat again. Madden got the ball over the plate, and Bench came through with yet another "on-demand" performance, smoking a home run to left (the 389th of his career) to make Johnny Bench Night an unforgettable experience for anyone who was there to witness it.

And what, by the way, do you get for the ballplayer who has enough money to buy whatever he wants? Who knows in this day of major league salaries that are the equivalent of the GNP of small countries, but here is a sample list of the gifts that the game's greatest backstop received on Johnny Bench Night:

- Fishing boat
- Wheelbarrow full of golf balls (one for each of Bench's career home runs)
- Sterling silver plate embedded with a number five made of rubies
- Golfing trip to Scotland
- New Ford Bronco

TODD BENZINGER

Todd Benzinger is remembered for catching the popup that ended the 1990 World Series, a startling four-game sweep by the Cincinnati Reds over the heavily favored Oakland A's. The triumph was sweet revenge for Benzinger, who had been a member of the Boston Red Sox squad, which itself had been swept by the A's in the 1988 American League Championship Series. Yet, contrary to popular speculation, Todd's moment in the World Series spotlight is not his most memorable moment in baseball.

"First of all, our victory over Oakland was not a fluke," says Benzinger. "We wouldn't have beaten them twenty out of twenty games, but we would have beaten them in every four-game series we played them. We weren't the most talented team in baseball—we weren't even in the top five—but we matched up well with Oakland. Sometimes that sort of thing just happens, especially in basketball. You think you're better than another team, but you lose because you don't match up well with them. Well, we matched up great with Oakland. For instance, the A's were good hitters, but they had trouble with pitchers like Jose Rijo because of the way he pitched. Tom Browning was not a great pitcher, but he was a fly ball pitcher who was the perfect guy for us to throw in Game Three at their place, because they have a big ballpark. They hit a lot of harmless, warning track fly balls against Browning. We had a lot of speed, working against a catcher with a mediocre arm. And we had a bullpen that was second to none, which I guess they weren't even thinking about. All these things added up to give us an advantage over them. And so, it wasn't as big an upset as everybody thinks it was. And, although I was thrilled to make the last play of that World Series, it probably wasn't as meaningful to me as it was to everybody else.

"As far as I'm concerned, the most memorable thing about my career was getting called up to the major leagues by the Boston Red Sox. I think a lot of players feel the same way, even players who go on to be big stars. There's just something about that moment when you get the call, when you know that all your hard work is finally going to pay off. It's such a thrill that it's almost surreal. It was a moment I'll never forget because for me it wasn't just being called up to the big leagues. It was being called up to Fenway Park to play for the Red Sox—on a Friday night in the middle of June, to play against the New York Yankees, who were in town for the first time that summer, with Roger Clemens on the mound to start the game for us. That's a cut above the typical experience in my book. I didn't get into the game that night, but I remember John McNamara, the Boston manager, asking me in the middle of the game, 'Well, how do you like the big leagues, young man?' All I could say was 'Pretty good, skip. Pretty good.'

"I didn't play the next day either, but I got into the third game on Sunday. Bob Tewksbury started for the Yankees and was pitching a great game. He was getting out Wade Boggs, Bill Buckner, Don Baylor, Jim Rice—all our great hitters. I pinch-hit for our catcher Marc Sullivan in the bottom of the seventh, with the Yankees winning 2–1, nobody on, and two outs. Tewksbury walked me on four pitches—not intentionally, but he pitched me very carefully. He did that because I'd hit a home run off him the year before in Triple A, and he remembered me. I'm sure the people in the stands, the Boston fans who are very knowledgeable, were wondering why Tewksbury pitched like that to me, a guy making his major league debut. I mean he didn't even throw me anything close to a strike. So Tewksbury put me on, and then Ellis Burks, the next batter, hit a home run to put us ahead. And I remember thinking how cool it was to walk in my first at-bat, to be shown that kind of respect when the pitcher was getting everybody else in the lineup out.

"The very best thing about my call up, though, was telephoning my dad to share the news with him. I'd never looked forward more to making a call to my dad than I did that day. My dad was a hardworking guy, who always worked two jobs, and a great baseball fan. He was very knowledgeable about baseball history because he read baseball books all the time, and he'd read the same book five or six times.

"Anyway, when I got drafted out of high school and left to go to Elmira, New York, to play minor league baseball, my dad, who was a man of few words, said, 'Step one, Son, step one.'

"The next year, in 1982, when he drove me to the airport for spring training, he said, 'Step two, Son, step two.' And every year he'd say I was taking another step. So, the great thing about it was that when I made that phone call to him to say I was going up to the big leagues, he said, 'Step six, Son. The last one. You did it!' And he was overjoyed to say it, too."

YOGI BERRA

No one in baseball has ever uttered more funny statements than Yogi Berra—the great Yankees catcher whose zany remarks have become known as "Yogi-isms." Berra claims that his humor is always unintentional. "Quotes just happen," he says. "When people ask me to say a Yogi-ism, I tell them that I don't make them up on the spot. If I could do that, I'd be famous."

We know what Yogi was trying to say there, but the fact remains that anyone who hangs around him for any length of time is going to pick up a Yogi-ism or two, as did Joe Altobelli, who joined Berra as a coach for the Yankees in 1981 after having served a stint as manager of the San Francisco Giants. At the time, the silly "streaking" craze had become popular at Comiskey Park. When the Yankees were preparing to make their first trip of the season to Chicago to play the White Sox, the topic of the exhibitionists who would run naked through the grandstands or across the field came up in conversation.

"Are most of the streakers male or female?" asked Altobelli.

"I don't know," said Yogi. "They always have paper bags over their heads."

BOOKS

As hard as it is to believe today, Roger Kahn's classic of baseball literature, *The Boys of Summer*, received more than a few bad reviews when it was first published in 1971. Fortunately, the snotty reviewers were far outnumbered by ordinary members of the reading public who completely embraced Kahn's searing before-and-after stories about members of the 1952–53 Brooklyn Dodgers—including Columbus Clippers radio broadcaster Gary Richards, who, as a fifteen-year-old in 1973, had the sense to recommend the book to his high school English teacher.

"I went to high school in Mecca, Ohio, right outside Youngstown," says Gary, "and one day when I was in ninth grade Mrs. Gates asked us what book we wanted to read as a class. Nobody said a thing, so I raised my hand and suggested that we read *The Boys of Summer*. I was reading the book at the time and was really moved by the Jackie Robinson part of the story. I'd been going through a school system that was all white from K through 12, and I thought that the book would provide some perspective for some of the rednecks in my class. Mrs. Gates hadn't heard of the book, so she said she'd have to take it home and read it. After she read it, she said she'd have to think about letting us read it as a class because she was worried about some of the language and the sex, which was really only the story about Roy Campanella's wife cheating on him. Ninth graders today wouldn't bat an eye over such mild content, but you have to realize that things were different back in 1973. Mrs. Gates decided to ask the principal, Mr. Zeller, about it, and fortunately he was a big baseball fan, so he gave her the okay.

"When the girls in the class found out we were going to be reading a baseball book, they whined and complained, but Mrs. Gates told them, 'This is a story within a story, and the most important things in the book are not necessarily about baseball.' Well, the girls quickly changed their minds, and they got really caught up in the book because many of the stories in *The Boys of Summer* are so touching, such as the one about Carl Erskine's learning-disabled son. And they discovered, as Mrs. Gates had discovered, that you don't have to be a big baseball fan to appreciate the book.

"When we finished *The Boys of Summer*, I guess I pushed my luck because I recommended that we read *Ball Four* next. Mrs. Gates said, 'We probably shouldn't read another baseball book.' Mr. Zeller, who knew what kind of baseball book *Ball Four* was, was even more adamant about it. It had a lot more of the sex and objectionable language that Mrs. Gates was worried about. He said, 'No way!' You can't blame a guy for trying, though. So the next book we read wasn't a baseball book. It was a pretty decent substitute, though: *The Martian Chronicles*, by Ray Bradbury."

B aseball is the most verbal of games. Chatter, storytelling, reminiscing, debate, and just plain conversation are tools of the game as essential as bats, balls, and gloves. Moreover, baseball language has never remained a thing apart but has always insinuated itself into the larger domain of American speech to a degree surpassed by few other activities. Over the years, the colorfulness and importance of baseball language have attracted a number of linguists, none more important than Paul Dickson, who in 1989 published the first edition of the greatest book on the subject, *The Dickson Baseball Dictionary*. While Dickson's book is amazingly comprehensive, students of the game with attentive ears can have a lot of fun playing amateur lexicographer, trying to find words, terms, and phrases not contained in Dickson; for example:

Casey Award—Established in 1983 and sponsored by *Spitball: The Literary Baseball Magazine*, the Casey is a bronze plaque awarded annually to the author of what is voted to be the best baseball book of the year. *The Dickson Baseball Dictionary* was nominated for the 1989 Casey Award.

credential—a recognition given to sportswriters and other working members of the media by baseball teams that allows the accredited media members access to the field, clubhouse, and press box; also, the paper or laminated card (usually hung around the neck by a cord or chain), which itself represents the recognition.

cut—the signature of a ballplayer or other baseball notable that is "cut" from a larger piece of paper.

duck fart—a current synonym for bloop hit or "dying quail."

first ballot—in reference to members of the National Baseball Hall of Fame who are elected in their inaugural year of eligibility.

in the bucket—an umpire's term meaning working the plate, not the bases.

pearl—a new, spotless, unsmudged baseball.

plaque—one of an ongoing series of postcards produced by the National Baseball Hall of Fame and Museum, each of which features a photo of one of the bronze plaques hanging in the Hall of Fame Gallery.

sleeves—a nickname for the undershirts the players wear. Sometimes the entire undershirt is colored; sometimes only the sleeves are.

strapping—another umpire's term meaning working the plate; in reference to the equipment the plate man has to put on.

As language is constantly changing, this is a game within the game that fans can enjoy playing as long as baseball comes up with new lingo and they have the ears to hear it.

Fans who were paying attention to major league baseball back in the 1960s and '70s will remember Wes Parker of the Los Angeles Dodgers because Parker did not fit the mold prescribed for the position he played. First base in the major leagues is normally reserved for good hitters or sluggers; but Parker, who batted .267 lifetime with a season high of 13 homers, was neither. So why was Parker the Dodgers' regular first baseman from 1964 through 1972? Because the Dodgers of his day relied on pitching and defense to win, and there wasn't a better first baseman alive than Wes Parker. In fact, based on his statistics, Parker ranks as one of the slickest fielders to ever play the game. He made just 49 errors during his nine-year career (all with the Dodgers), won six consecutive Gold Gloves, and finished with a fielding average of .995. Another peculiarity about the switch-hitting Parker was the fact that in 1965 and 1966, when the Dodgers won National League pennants, he combined with second baseman Jim Lefebvre, shortstop Maury Wills, and third baseman Jim Gilliam to form the only switch-hitting infield in major league history.

After he hung up his spikes, the handsome Parker, who took up broadcasting and acting, did not experience the usual difficulty that most major league players have in adjusting to life without baseball. In fact, Parker always had many outside interests and involvements, and it was his preoccupation with them that kept him from realizing his full potential as a hitter. As an experiment, Parker decided in 1970 to devote his full attention to baseball for one season. The result was the best year of his career: 196 hits, 111 RBI, and a .319 average (all of them team highs), in addition to a league high of 47 doubles.

Today, Wes Parker continues to defy the conventional image of a professional athlete in that he is passionate not only about reading, but about book collecting as well. An Ernest Hemingway and John Steinbeck collector, Parker once owned the country's best collection of books by novelist Ian Fleming, the creator of British spy James Bond, Agent 007. Parker proudly put together a first edition collection of all American and British Fleming books in both hard cover and paperback that included signed copies of the twelve James Bond novels published during Fleming's lifetime. (The last two Bond novels were published posthumously.)

Not surprisingly, Parker currently has the baseball book bug, and his collection of books about the National Pastime includes more than seven hundred volumes. "At first, I just collected books I thought I'd like," he says, "but then I found out about *Diamond Classics: Essays on 100 of the Best Baseball Books Ever Published* and the Casey Awards, which I use as tools to give my baseball book collecting focus. I'm trying to acquire a first edition copy of every book in *Diamond Classics* and every book that has won or been nominated for the Casey Award. At this point I'm only missing six of the one hundred books in *Diamond Classics*."

Parker's favorite baseball book? That would be Douglas Wallop's novel based on the Faustian legend, *The Year the Yankees Lost the Pennant*. "It's a wonderful story," says Parker, "and very well written. It focuses on the Yankees, the team everybody either loves or hates with a passion, and it revolves around the fantasy that every fan has had: to be a great slugger. Plus, it was the first baseball book I ever read."

Parker's least favorite type of baseball book is autobiographies. "They're all about one player and his gripes," he says. "There are exceptions, but I usually find them to be self-serving." Despite his disdain for the genre, Parker is working on a book about his own career, which he promises will be only partially autobiographical. "I want to talk as much about all the great players I played with and against as I want to talk about myself," he says. In the meantime, he is continuing to build a first-class library of baseball books and continuing to enhance his status as a unique baseball bibliophile who combines literary acumen with real-life major league playing experience.

BRET BOONE

After Bret Boone of the Seattle Mariners turned in one of the greatest years a second baseman has ever had in major league history (.331, 37, 141) in 2001, some observers may have felt that he had enjoyed a cakewalk to such success. After all, Boone's father, Bob, and grandfather, Ray, had both been successful major league ballplayers. Bret's distinguished lineage, however, did not guarantee his own place in the big leagues. Rather, Bret earned it through hard work and determination. In fact, his desire was so manifest that it made a lasting impression on everyone who watched him play in the minor leagues; including Peter Bragan Jr., general manager of the Double-A Jacksonville Suns, for whom Boone played in 1991. "Boone wasn't that good of a hitter when he was here," says Bragan. "He lunged at the ball a lot; and, as good a hitter as he's become, he still does that today some. But, boy, was he a gamer! He was tough as nails and never came out of the lineup. When he'd get hurt, he'd just put a Band-Aid on it and go. He was never the most talented player; he just willed himself to become a big leaguer.

"Something else motivated Boone, too. He wanted to be the first third-generation player to get to the big leagues. In fact, he made a bet with Jim Campanis's son, another third-generation player who was also on our team that year, as to which one of them would make it first. As it turned out, their bet wasn't a contest.

"See, Campanis met this girl here at the beginning of the year. She had dark hair and dark eyes and was a real beauty. She was a hottie and hot-tempered too—she and Campanis had some arguments, let me tell you. But he fell in love with her, and they got married here on the diamond, with the other players holding up baseball bats to form a canopy for them to walk under—the whole bit. They got married on get-away day and then couldn't be together after the ceremony because the team was riding a bus up to Greenville or Richmond or some place like that. Our policy was not to let wives and girlfriends ride the bus because our insurance didn't cover them, so she followed the bus in her car.

"The next year Boone started in Triple A, had a great year there, and was even promoted to Seattle at the end of the season. Campanis was back with us that spring, and by then he not only had a young wife but a new baby as well. His mind wasn't always on the game as it should have been. You could look at him and tell that he was thinking about things like buying diapers, not baseball. So he washed out at Double A and never did get to the big leagues. From the first moment Campanis saw her, he had his eye on that girl. Boone kept his eye on the ball."

LARRY BOWA

Larry Bowa, the current manager of the Philadelphia Phillies, may have been a runt of a ballplayer, but he was one of the best fielding shortstops of his day, and through hard work and determination he made himself into a pretty fair hitter, too, accumulating almost 2,200 hits during his sixteen-year major league career.

After establishing himself as a big leaguer, Bowa took his accomplishments in stride; however, as Bill Schlesinger recalls, in the minor leagues Bowa got school-boyishly excited about his big days at the ballpark.

"In 1969 when I played for the Phillies' Triple-A team in Eugene, Oregon, we were loaded," says Schlesinger. "Mike Schmidt, Greg Luzinski, Denny Doyle, Larry Bowa, and I all played on that team, and Larry and I roomed together. Now Larry only weighed about 125 pounds, and he could hit the ball about 150 feet at the farthest. But he was a terrific fielder, he had a great arm at short, and he was tough—had a little Pete Rose in him as far as being a competitor goes.

"Larry loved to see his name in the paper, loved to read nice write-ups about himself in the paper, and whenever he had a good game and thought the writers would mention him he would buy five or six copies of the paper to send back home to his parents and his girlfriend, I guess. He'd be so excited he could hardly sleep, and he'd get up at seven or eight o'clock in the morning just to check out the paper and to be sure that he'd be able to buy some extra copies of it. This was unusual behavior for a ballplayer because most players don't care what the papers say about them, and they certainly aren't going to get up early to buy a newspaper. Heck, most players don't ever get out of bed after a night game until noon. But Larry, he'd be up at the crack of dawn in order to read about himself.

"Well, one night he had the best game of his career. I think he went five for five, with two doubles, two triples, and a home run—he was usually good for two or three extra base hits a month—and he made a couple of sensational plays in the field to boot. In the clubhouse after the game he was really excited. He said, 'I think I might get headlines for that game. Heck, I might even get headlines on the front page of the entire paper, not just the sports page! Bill, do you think I'll get headlines?'

"'You should,' I said. 'You had a great night. It was "Bowa Night" at the ballpark.'

"Later on he started feeling a little embarrassed about getting so excited, and he quit talking about being in the newspaper, but I knew it was still on his mind, so I decided to play a little prank on him. We went to bed about two, as usual, but around four thirty in the morning I got up without waking him. I went down into the lobby, waited around until the newspapers were delivered, and then got the desk clerk to let me buy all one hundred copies. They were about twenty cents each back then, so it cost me twenty dollars. Then I took them upstairs and piled them right outside our door, in about three big piles, so that when the door was opened they'd spill into the room. Then I went back to sleep, knowing exactly what Bowa was going to do.

"Sure enough, he woke up about seven thirty and started getting dressed, and I woke up, too. 'What are you doing up so early?' I asked him.

"'Oh, I don't know,' he said. 'I'm just restless. I might go for a walk.'

"'Yeah, right,' I said. 'A walk to the lobby.'

"He acted like he didn't know what I was talking about and headed out of the room. As soon as he opened the door, those stacks of newspapers fell into the room right on top of his shoes. He started laughing and said, 'You big ass!'

"'What?' I said. 'I'm just saving you a trip downstairs and the trouble of hauling all those papers up here. My only concern is did I get enough for you?' He laughed some more about that. And yes, he did make headlines. I think he got the message, too, because he kind of cooled it after that with the newspapers."

MARTY BRENNAMAN

Baseball is the best game in the world to listen to on radio, especially if the broadcaster is as good as the Cincinnati Reds' longtime play-by-play man, Marty Brennaman. Reds fans love Brennaman for his objectivity, his candor, his sense of humor, and, above all, his ability to always keep the game interesting. Having a good-natured putdown or a funny story handy whenever the game hits a lull is one way Brennaman keeps things interesting, but his ace in the hole is his inventiveness with the language.

For instance, in Brennaman-speak, a "three-run Johnson" is a home run with two runners on base. In his postgame wrap-up, Marty doesn't tell us how many people were at the game; he announces the attendance for "this titanic struggle." Striking out four times in a single game merits a player the "golden sombrero," as in "Ellis Burks is going for the golden sombrero." When someone is visibly upset about something, he has a bad case of the "goo-goos," and when the Reds get behind and need a comeback, "That's a big old HWE [hang with 'em]." Even when Brennaman isn't coining words and phrases, he is able to put his stamp on the broadcast just with the tone of his voice, as when he concludes a conversation with utter finality by saying "Thank you!" to mean "I agree, and that's the end of that."

As fun as it is to follow Brennaman's verbal adventures, Reds fans love most of all to hear the statement, "And this one belongs to the Reds!" which has been for almost three decades Marty's way of saying that the team has just won another ballgame. The statement is Brennaman's signature and is as well known to Reds fans as the wishbone "C" on the team's uniforms, yet it caused a bit of controversy in early 2003 as the Reds hurried to finish the construction of their new ballpark in time for Opening Day.

Brennaman's longtime partner in the radio booth is former Reds pitcher Joe Nuxhall, who has a trademark signoff that he uses at the end of the broadcast: "This is the old left-hander rounding third and heading for home." To honor Nuxhall, the Reds hung the phrase "Rounding third and heading for home" in red neon lights on the outside wall of the new Great American Ballpark. When asked if the team was planning to do the same for Brennaman, chief operating officer John Allen said no, they were not. According to Allen, a representative of Hamilton County—Allen couldn't remember exactly who the representative was—had nixed the idea in a meeting held a couple of years earlier on the basis that the public would interpret the sign as a message from the Reds claiming that the new ballpark, built at taxpayers' expense, belonged to the team.

When word of this got out, Reds fans barraged county offices with protests at the dim-wittedness of the ban; county officials backtracked as quickly as possible; and Brennaman, never one to mince words, made his opinion on the subject clear. "For them to say people are going to confuse my phrase with the Reds saying that the ballpark belongs to them is ridiculous," he said. "I say, 'This one belongs to the Reds,' not 'This ballpark belongs to the Reds.' I've been using it for twenty-nine seasons. Anybody who's a Reds fan knows it is my signature phrase. It's indicative of the small-town thinking being done by the county."

The flap died down when county officials asserted that they had no objection to the Reds making use of Brennaman's words at the new ballpark in any way they deemed fit. In the end, the whole "titanic struggle" was nothing but a case of the "googoos." Before county officials donned "golden sombreros," they came to their senses and agreed with the rest of us that "this one [a well-deserved honor] belongs to Marty!" "Thank you."

TOM BROWNING

Tom Browning is as human as the rest of us, but he deserves his nickname, "Mr. Perfect," which he earned when he pitched the only thing better than a no-hitter on September 16, 1988. Browning's perfect game, only the sixteenth in major league history, came against the Los Angeles Dodgers and put him in the company of some of the game's greatest hurlers: Cy Young, Jim Bunning, Sandy Koufax, and Catfish Hunter. The game was played at Cincinnati's Riverfront Stadium, and rain postponed the start of the game until ten o'clock. Browning made such quick work of the Dodgers that the game was over before midnight. "My control that night was so good it was—well, perfect," says Browning. "I wasn't a power pitcher so I always relied on location, deception, changes of speed, things like that; and I'd usually make some mistakes when the hitters would hurt me, but not that night. Everything I threw went right where it was supposed to, and if I did make any mistakes the batters just didn't hit them for some reason. My control was so good I don't think I even went to three balls on a single batter. Also, you usually need some help from your defense to pitch a game like that, or to even come close to it, but everything was pretty routine for the guys behind me. It was just one of those nights."

If Browning's defense didn't make any great plays to save his perfect game, they also, on the other hand, didn't make any errors that would have ruined his perfecto. And Browning, like all pitchers, certainly had his days when the fielders behind him let him down.

"One day when I was pitching against the Cubs at Wrigley Field," says Mr. Perfect, "the defense behind me was terrible. The guys made errors all over the place—couldn't catch anything. I got beat 4–3, and all the runs were unearned. After the game I went out to dinner with my roommate, Rick Stowe, who was in charge of our clubhouse back home. Rick and I were walking down the street in Chicago on the way to our favorite restaurant when this panhandler came up to us. The guy asked me for money, and I said, 'Leave me alone. I've had a terrible day, and I'm in a bad mood.'

"The guy didn't want to take no for an answer, so he held up his hands and said, 'Come on, man. Look at these hands!' His hands were awful looking—all scaly and blotchy as if he had leprosy or something.

"I said, 'Yeah, so what. Those are the best hands I've seen all day.'

"Rick laughed at that, I went ahead and gave the poor guy twenty dollars, and I started to feel a little better about the ball-game and all those errors I'd been victimized by."

CASEY CANDAELE

Although he spent parts of nine seasons with the Montreal Expos, Houston Astros, and Cleveland Indians, infielder Casey Candaele became a legend in the minor leagues—as a prankster and a comic. Candaele, whose mother, the former Helen St. Aubin, played professional baseball during World War II in the All-American Girls Baseball League, never lost an opportunity to amuse his teammates, especially during road trips when mind-numbing boredom becomes enemy number one for ballplayers.

Former Cleveland Indians pitcher Tom Kramer tells a story about the time Candaele cracked up his teammates on the Triple-A Buffalo Bisons by going to extremes to best Cal Ripken's little brother, Billy, in a most unusual contest.

"I don't know who started this thing," says Kramer, "and it could have been Billy Ripken because he was as nutty as Casey. At any rate, the two of them got involved in this contest to see which of them could travel the lightest. Every road trip the team took the two of them kept showing up with fewer and fewer suitcases and then smaller and smaller suitcases.

"One day the guys were sitting around the airport terminal, killing time before they could board their flight, when Casey showed up. He was walking real slow and stiffly and had his arms out away from his sides. He looked as puffed up as the Michelin Man because he was wearing all the clothes he was taking on the road trip—six pairs of underwear, four pairs of pants, seven or eight shirts, six or seven pairs of socks—and the only traveling bag he had in his hand was a little toiletry bag.

"Ripken took one look at him and said, 'Okay. That's it. You win.'"

SEAN CASEY

Although Sean Casey is a very talented player, what has endeared him to the fans of the Cincinnati Reds, as well as to his teammates, is his personality and his character. A devout Christian, Casey lives by the Golden Rule and endeavors at all times to treat everyone else as he would like to be treated. He also plays with an infectious optimism and a big kid's love of the game that makes him a pleasure to be around.

Casey immediately showed Cincinnati what kind of special person and player he was by the way he reacted when an injury at the beginning of his rookie year almost ended his career before it got started. Casey, who had been traded to the Reds by Cleveland less than twenty-four hours before the start of the 1998 season, was helping the middle infielders work on double plays during batting practice before the third game of the season, on April 2, when a throw from second baseman Damian Jackson hit him flush in the right eye. Casey suffered a gushing cut that required twenty stitches to close and an orbital fracture that affected four bones around his eye. This grisly injury reminded observers of eye accidents that cut short the highly promising careers of Boston's Tony Conigliaro and Cleveland's Herb Score; but Casey turned out to be more fortunate than either of those star-crossed players. His vision returned almost immediately and was normal except for one thing: the double vision he had when he moved his eye upward.

Specialists operated on Casey on April 8 and repaired the broken bones by inserting a plate held in place by five screws. The procedure not only cured Casey's double vision, but it also

improved his vision to the point that he was later able to discard the contact lenses he'd worn before the injury. Remarkably, Casey was back in uniform by April 30. He struggled for a while and endured a career-worst 0-for-25 slide; but he became the Reds' regular first baseman on June 19, and by the end of the season he had raised his average to a respectable .272.

As courageous as this comeback was, it was Casey's concern and compassion for another victim of an eye injury similar to his own that really showed his true colors.

The following year on April 23 Anthony Molina of the University of Evansville was hit in the eye while standing near the batter's box waiting to lead off a game against Wichita State University. After reading about Molina's injury in *Baseball America*, Casey obtained Molina's phone number and called the junior first baseman to give him a little pep talk.

Understandably, Molina was depressed about his injury; but Casey, who empathized with him the way no one else could, encouraged him not to give up. Molina later told the *Evansville Courier and Press* that Casey "just kept saying that everything happens for a reason, and that the important thing is where I go from here." By the end of the conversation with Casey, Molina did feel better. After all, he realized that Casey had more to offer than his prayers and well wishes. Casey, who had started the 1999 season hot as a firecracker and would wind up fourth in batting in the National League, was offering the kid hope that his recovery would be as complete as his own had been.

HOPALONG CASSADY

Ohio State University halfback Howard "Hopalong" Cassady won the 1955 Heisman Trophy, college football's most prestigious honor. But few people outside of Columbus, Ohio, realize that Cassady also has a baseball background. "Hop," as he is known to friends, played baseball at Ohio State with Frank Howard, who went on to enjoy a long career as a feared slugger in the major leagues, and he played semipro baseball with legendary University of Michigan football coach Bo Schembechler. Cassady has also had a relationship with the New York Yankees for more than three decades; a relationship that had its origins with Yankees owner George Steinbrenner. Then an assistant football coach at Purdue, Steinbrenner was the one who first informed Cassady that he had won the Heisman. Since 1992 Cassady has served as the first base coach for the Columbus Clippers, the Yankees' Triple-A farm team in the International League.

Despite Cassady's considerable experience in professional baseball, it is his status as a Heisman Trophy winner that is constantly on everyone's mind, as the following story told by Clippers historian Joe Santry illustrates.

"Although Hop is a living legend here in Columbus," says Santry, "he's also the warmest, sweetest, most loving guy you'd ever want to meet. And he's so modest that you'd never know that he was a Heisman Trophy winner. I think he uses his Heisman Trophy as a doorstop in his granddaughter's bedroom.

"As you know, the Ohio State football team won the national championship in 2002, so the team's coach, Jim Tressel, was asked to throw out the ceremonial first pitch at the Clippers' Opening Day Game in 2003. Tressel was going to throw the first pitch to our manager Bucky Dent, but before he did he reached down into a bag he'd carried out to the mound. He pulled out a football, called out to Hop, and waved him up to home plate from a circle of on-lookers. I was standing nearby taking photos, and when I realized what was happening I said a prayer to myself: 'Please, Lord. Don't let Hop drop this pass and get embarrassed in front of this sell-out crowd.' I mean, Hop was a great athlete, but he's sixty-nine years old now.

"When Tressel threw the football, Hop spun sideways, reached up over his head like a wide receiver, and made a perfect catch. And then, before I could even go 'Whew!' in relief, he struck the famous ball-carrier-in-motion Heisman Trophy pose with his head turned to the right toward the grandstands, the ball tucked in his left arm, and his right hand extended in a classic stiff arm. The explosion from the crowd was so loud that it literally shook the ballpark. It was a wonderful, entirely unscripted moment—which, needless to say, completely upstaged the official ceremonial first pitch."

COLLECTING

The first bobbing-head dolls were papier-mâché baseball team figures made in Japan in the early 1960s. Also called "bobbers," these dolls featured either a generic boy head, always with a cherubic face, or a team mascot head that was attached by a spring to a chubby body dressed in the uniform of the major league team being represented. When tapped lightly, the head of the doll would bob up and down enthusiastically, hence the name.

These cheap souvenirs, originally costing between one and three dollars, did not sell well at first but became highly sought-after and expensive collectibles in the 1980s. In the early 1990s new bobbers, this time representing individual players instead of teams, were produced and became quite popular. When major league teams began giving away player-specific bobbing-head dolls as special promotions in the late 1990s, bobbers became a certified collecting craze. It was not at all unusual for fans to line up hours before a game to make sure they received a bobber, and prices for such bobbers often skyrocketed on the Internet before the games at which they were distributed were concluded.

Bobbing-head-doll mania spread beyond baseball to encompass other sports and even nonsport professions, such as politics (e.g., President George W. Bush) and the music industry (e.g, Ozzie Osborne). Some observers felt that the craze reached its outer limits, though, at the National Sports Collectors Convention in 2002, where a baseball-card dealer introduced a bobbing-head doll, not of a slugger in the major leagues or of a famous NFL quarterback, but of himself.

At first glance, a bobbing-head doll of a bald-headed, four-eyed, middle-aged baseball-card dealer may seem ridiculous; but

Alan Rosen is not your average card dealer, and there is definitely a method to the madness of an Alan Rosen bobbing-head doll.

Alan Rosen came to the baseball-card hobby from the coin business around 1978, a time that now seems like the hobby's prehistoric era. The baseball-card hobby was so innocent and undeveloped that collectors and dealers alike had almost no concept of the importance of condition, which had long been the key factor in the pricing of rare coins. Rosen changed that forever by always demanding that the cards he bought be nothing but mint condition specimens. His insistence on top-grade cards revolutionized the hobby and earned him the nickname "Mr. Mint."

Rosen realized that there was a lot of money to be made in buying the highest quality cards and reselling them for premium prices based on their condition, and he dove into the business of doing so with great energy, shrewdness, and a genius for promotion. Rosen spent big bucks on advertising, and his ubiquitous full-page ads in leading hobby publications such as *Sports Collectors Digest* have always been centered around one thing: a photo of Mr. Mint himself, flashing a big smile and even bigger wads of cash to prospective sellers. Thousands of sellers have gotten the message over the years, and no one has made more "big buys" in the hobby than Mr. Mint.

So, why a bobbing-head doll self-portrait? "Well, I'm a promotion guy," says Rosen. "I believe that getting a picture of my mug out there keeps me ahead of the other dealers." And since bobbing-head dolls were the hottest thing in the hobby in 2002, it only made sense, at least to Rosen, for him to have a Mr. Mint bobber available to give away to prospective customers at the hobby's biggest annual event. After all, there has been a Mr. Mint give-away item available for the past eighteen national conventions. In fact, one could at this point assemble a pretty interesting collection of Mr. Mint items, consisting of such things

as a key chain, a pennant, a trading card, a photo baseball, and a beanie baby. The ceaseless self-promotion represented by such items may irk some observers, but there's no arguing with success. If creating a Mr. Mint bobber is the price he has to pay—2,500 bobbers at $4 a piece—Alan Rosen is willing to pay it. Like any savvy politician, Mr. Mint knows the value of name-and-face recognition. "I don't care what you say about me, as long as you spell my name right," he says. That's M-R. M-I-N-T!

Just when baseball card collectors thought they'd seen it all, along came the Topps Company with perhaps the most radical idea to ever hit the hobby: baseball cards that you buy but don't physically possess. Topps, which has a long history of producing experimental products, really went to bat without a helmet in 2001 with the creation of eTopps cards; but the concept, as crazy as it sounds, appears to have a chance of catching on.

What exactly are eTopps cards? Quite simply, they are guaranteed mint-condition state-of-the-art cards that combine two of the hottest developments in American society in the 1990s: the Internet and the stock market.

eTopps cards are related to the Internet in that they can originally be purchased only online directly from Topps. The cards, which come sealed in plastic cases, actually exist; but as they are meant to remain stored in a Topps warehouse, they are akin to virtual cards, which would exist only in cyberspace. In addition, the eTopps website is linked to eBay in order to help collectors buy and sell cards from one another.

The influence of the stock market can be seen in eTopps lingo. The cards are made available, six at a time, during "IPOs" (initial player offerings), which last only a week. The print run for each new card is announced, and the cards not sold during the IPO are destroyed to preserve the scarcity and enhance the value of the remaining cards. In addition, collectors who purchase eTopps cards (IPO prices range from $4 to $9.50 per card) build a "portfolio," the value of which they can check anytime online and which is based on the most recent auction resells of the cards they also own.

Collectors can opt to have the eTopps cards they purchase shipped to them by Topps for a small fee. But in surrendering to the old-fashioned need to handle his cards, the collector removes the cards from his online portfolio and technically eliminates the very "E"lectronic essence of the cards. Such complications may thrill collectors who welcome this "Brave New World" of card collecting, but they certainly dismay others who yearn for the days when baseball cards were made of cheap cardboard, cost a penny a piece, and came with something you could really sink your teeth into: a powdery stick of sugary pink gum!

T he most famous private collection of baseball memorabilia was that of Barry Halper, a minority owner of the New York Yankees who spent almost five decades amassing such an astonishing assemblage of rarities that only the collection of the National Baseball Hall of Fame in Cooperstown could rival it. When Halper turned to Sotheby's for help with liquidating his massive holdings, the auction turned into the most spectacular event in hobby history. The auction ran for one solid week, from September 23 through 29, 1999. Close to 2,500 lots were put up for bid, and the three-volume auction catalog ran to nine hundred pages. Winning bids routinely skyrocketed past their estimates; and when the smoke cleared, more than $22 million had been spent.

All of the hobby's heavy hitters participated in the auction, as did several celebrities, such as actor-comedian Billy Crystal, who snagged a 1960 game-worn fielders' glove that had once belonged to his hero, Mickey Mantle, for a mere $239,000.

It wasn't the Mantle glove that received the most attention, though. Nor was it any of the other fantastic items, such as Lou Gehrig's 1927 World Series ring, Ted Williams's Triple Crown Award, or an autographed Willie Mays jersey from his rookie year. No, the piece that mesmerized the media was the oddest and ugliest item in the auction: Ty Cobb's dentures. The false teeth, which came with Cobb's original plaster denture holder, itself affixed to a brass opening device, had been left by Cobb to his biographer, Al Stump. Sotheby's guessed that the dentures would go for between three and five hundred dollars, but that estimate would prove to be exceedingly low, thanks to a Clark's Summit, Pennsylvania, homemaker named Karen Shemonsky.

Shemonsky, who had never participated in an auction before, read about Ty Cobb's dentures in a *Business Week* magazine article in the spring of 1999 and decided she had to have them. "My father had been a dentist, from the old school," she says, "and I grew up around false teeth like Ty Cobb's. They just intrigued me." The dentures also appealed to Shemonsky because she felt that they would be within her reach, financially, unlike items associated with her lifelong hero, Mickey Mantle.

Once the auction started and she saw how often the bidding zoomed far beyond the estimated values of the items, Shemonsky, who was going to bid by phone, kept mentally raising her personal ceiling. Lot No. 1230 went up for bid on Monday, September 27th. By the time Sotheby's reached her over the phone, the bidding was already at $2,000. Flush with auction fever, Shemonsky plunged into the action and stayed in until she was declared the winner, at $7,475. With commission and sales tax the total wound up being $8,091.

Karen was immediately hounded by the media. "I had one of the most exciting weeks of my life," she says. "The phone rang off the hook for three days, and I did more than twenty phone interviews." Although the furor eventually died down, the dentures retained an amazing appeal. The History Channel came calling and interviewed Shemonsky about Ty's false teeth, and both the National Baseball Hall of Fame in Cooperstown and the Ty Cobb Museum in Royston, Georgia, have borrowed the dentures for exhibitions. As for Shemonsky, she has no regrets about spending so much money on an item far too tacky to ever be featured in an issue of *Good Housekeeping*. "Buying Ty Cobb's teeth is the best thing I ever did," she says. "The media loves them, and they should because they are so unique. George Washington's are the only other false teeth close to them in importance. I never dreamed I'd have so much fun owning them." Karen plans to leave the famous dentures to her sons, Brian and Chris, but they will have to wait until she has passed on. Right now, as Shemonsky says, "I'm having a ball!"

O f the more than ten thousand different sets of baseball cards that have been issued over the years, Little Sun's 1990 "Major League Writers" set is one of the most unusual. The set champions twenty-three of baseball's most important word-smiths, including cards of literary baseball pioneers Henry Chadwick, Jacob C. Morse, and Grantland Rice, as well as cards of contemporary stalwarts, such as Roger Kahn, John Holway, and

Peter Golenbock. An example of nearly every type of baseball writer is included, from newspaper reporter (Dick Young) to biographer (Robert Creamer) to historian (Harold Seymour) to poet (Tom Clark) to novelist (W. P. Kinsella) to screenwriter (Ron Shelton). While the set is not worth big bucks, its cultural importance is recognized by the leading voice of the baseball card hobby, *Sports Collectors Digest*, which includes "Major League Writers" in its mammoth *Standard Catalog of Baseball Cards*.

The most valuable cards in the set? According to the *Standard Catalog of Baseball Cards*, they would be the cards of the two writers in the set who played major league baseball before they picked up their pens: Jim Bouton, the author of *Ball Four*, and Jim Brosnan, the author of *The Long Season* and *Pennant Race*. Brosnan, who really got into the spirit of the project, gets extra credit for the photo on the front of his card. In it, Broz is standing on the mound in a minor league ballpark—smoking a pipe, wearing a coat and tie, and taking notes!

When it comes to famed American ingenuity, baseball collectors take a back seat to no one. Take, for example, the case of stadium seat collector George Tahan, whose love of seats from old ballparks has led him to invent one of the hottest new collectibles: miniature replicas of chairs from classic ballparks called "miniseats."

Tahan's idea for miniseats came to him in two stages. One day, when he was rearranging some of his full-size ballpark seats in his apartment, he noticed a baseball he'd caught at a Red Sox game sitting in one of his Comiskey Park seats. Although the

Comiskey Park seat dwarfed the baseball, Tahan liked how they looked together and thought "Wouldn't it be great to have a smaller, authentic-looking stadium chair into which a baseball fit perfectly?" Such miniseats would work especially well, he thought, as holders for autographed baseballs. And, they would be quite superior to the host of generic (mostly plastic) ball holders on the market in the sense that collectors could accommodate an autographed ball in a miniseat representing the ballpark associated with that player's team.

Tahan revisited the idea a few years later when he and his wife, Siobhan, were planning their wedding reception. "Instead of using the usual little placards to identify the tables in the hall, we thought it would be cool to put a small, numbered ballpark seat on each table," says Tahan, "with each number representing a famous ballplayer—for example, Table 8 would be the Carl Yastrzemski table." Tahan fashioned a prototype miniseat in his basement, but it unfortunately wasn't ready for prime time nuptials. Nevertheless, the experience convinced Tahan that the idea was feasible, and he became determined to one day turn the idea into reality.

Using his summer vacations from his job as the athletic director at Belmont Hill prep school outside of Boston, Tahan gradually perfected the production aspects of his miniseats with help from several professionals in the manufacturing fields. The first miniseats to be produced were the ones replicating seats from Yankee Stadium, Fenway Park, and Cleveland's Municipal Stadium. Tahan knew he was onto something right after he closed his first deal with Twins Souvenirs, located across the street from Fenway Park. "I sold them twenty-five Fenway Park miniseats," says George, "and they called me the next day to reorder. Red Sox employees discovered them and bought out the whole initial order."

The miniseats became so popular so quickly that Tahan also began production of Ebbets Field, Wrigley Field, Forbes Field, and Crosley Field miniseats. Comiskey Park, Tiger Stadium, and Griffith Stadium miniseats are next in the production pipeline. Tahan's miniseats appeal to a broad range of baseball collectors, but they are a godsend to serious collectors of full-sized ballpark seats—which, after all, take up a lot of room and can quickly elbow a collector out of his own house. No one knows this better than Tahan, a ballpark expert who calls his passion for research and tracking down unrecognized gems of stadia memorabilia "a kind of urban archaeology." Tahan himself wrestles with his collection of more than 125 full-sized ballpark seats; a collection that has filled the basement, the two-car garage, a locked room under his porch, and the entire third floor of his house. While there is always room for one more full-sized ballpark seat in Tahan's collection, for now he is concentrating on his miniseats, which are becoming a big deal in the collecting hobby.

FANS

Presumably, all fans help the teams they root for. Still, some fans make a greater contribution to the overall atmosphere at the games than others. For instance, take John Adams, a native Clevelander who has made his presence heard at nearly every Indians home game for the past thirty years.

A data systems analyst by profession, Adams has been sitting in the bleachers at Indians games since 1973, trying to keep his beloved Tribe on the warpath by rhythmically beating a bass drum throughout the game, especially in the late innings and whenever the team gets runners into scoring position. Adams, who is a real drummer by the way, began his unique avocation while in high school. Back then his favorite player, Rocky Colavito, patrolled the meadow in front of the right-field bleachers. "I never planned on doing this for thirty years," says Adams. "It just happened."

If the Indians' front office appreciates Adams's efforts, they have a funny way of showing it. Asked if the Indians give him his tickets, Adams said, "Yeah, they give me tickets. Then I give them money." Actually, Adams buys two season tickets: one for himself and one for his big drum. The Indians may keep their distance from Adams because a few people, such as the killjoy who wrote a letter to the editor saying that Adams ought to be fined for mocking Native American culture, have opposed his drumming due to a desire to adhere to a politically correct position. In any event, Adams remains undeterred and unapologetic. "Indians don't own a corner on drums," he says. "Drums have been used throughout history and in numerous cultures for communication and for calling people together." Such independent thinking is to be expected from a person who says he thinks that Alfred E. Neuman, the moronic figurehead of *Mad* magazine, would be a great presidential candidate. "My motto for Alfred E. Neuman's candidacy would be 'You could do worse . . . and you always have,'" jokes Adams.

Despite the disapproval of a few party poopers, Adams has practically become an institution at Indians games. Longtime Cleveland broadcaster Herb Score christened Adams "Big Chief Boom Boom," Adams is frequently asked for his autograph ("I'll sign anything but a blank check," he says), and fans constantly beg to be given the honor of beating his drum. "I tell 'em not to bother me when I'm playing, when I'm into the game," he says. "And I tell 'em they get one hit. Some people know how to count to one better than others."

The ultimate compliment for Adams came from Indians slugger Jim Thome, who said, "We know we're playing at home when we hear the drum." That recognition is enough to keep a dedicated fan going for three decades and counting.

The athletic supporter worn by Eddie Gaedel, the only midget to ever bat in an official major league baseball game. A partially smoked cigar left by Babe Ruth in a Philadelphia brothel. A heat-warped 45 rpm phonograph record salvaged from the "Disco Demolition Night" bonfire at Comiskey Park that caused the White Sox to forfeit a game on July 12, 1979. A fragment of skin from the inner left thigh of Abner Doubleday, the Civil War general who supposedly invented baseball in

1839. A satin thong panty that Boston Red Sox third baseman Wade Boggs insisted his mistress Margo Adams wear every day during one of his week-long batting streaks in 1986.

Such amazing, dare we say, unbelievable artifacts are not to be found at the grandest and most glorious institution for the preservation of baseball history, the National Baseball Hall of Fame and Museum in Cooperstown, New York. These wonders and more, however, are part of the collection of an alternative baseball museum called The Baseball Reliquary, Inc. Founded in 1996 by "super fan" Terry Cannon of Monrovia, California, The Baseball Reliquary is a nonprofit, educational organization whose mission, as stated in the organization's "Guide to the Collections," is to foster "an appreciation of the historical development of baseball and its interaction with American culture by the preservation and exhibition of artifacts related to the National Pastime." Such a declaration sounds perfectly normal, even prosaic, but is hardly the whole story. To get that, you must do a little reading between the lines.

Not to be glossed over is the organization's admission that it has "pursued a more visionary acquisitions policy" than other baseball museums. Even more telling is the statement in "Guide to the Collections," that "While each artifact is approached with meticulous scholarship and veracity, the ability of an object to invoke a sense of wonderment in, and to inspire the imagination of, the viewer is of supreme importance." A policy such as this would not hamper Ripley's Believe It Or Not in the least, but if any further evidence of The Baseball Reliquary's tongue-in-cheek tone is needed, consider the organization's name. The word *reliquary* means a storehouse of relics. A "relic" is a holy object that is treasured because it was once connected to a saint, but con artists of the Middle Ages routinely took advantage of believers by selling them fake relics. Thus, embedded in the word *relic* is a history of chicanery and deception, so it might seem that the very name of The Baseball Reliquary gives fair warning to all.

While skeptics may look askance at some of the fascinating artifacts in The Reliquary's ever-growing collection, the organization definitely takes seriously the role of educating the public; which it attempts to fulfill through an ongoing series of lectures and exhibitions and, especially, its annual Shrine of the Eternals program.

Unlike the Baseball Hall of Fame in Cooperstown, The Baseball Reliquary does not emphasize statistical accomplishment on the field of play as a criterion for election into its Shrine of the Eternals. Potential electees are judged on their "uniqueness of character and personality" and should be people who "have been responsible for developing baseball in one or more of the following ways: through athletic and/or business achievements; in terms of the larger cultural and sociological impact as a mass entertainment; and as an arena for the human imagination." Thus, players good, bad, and mediocre are eligible for enshrinement, but so are all sorts of people who would never be eligible for election to Cooperstown: authors, artists, fans of all stripes, and even fictional characters, such as George Plimpton's mythical pitcher with the 168-mph fastball, Sidd Finch! In addition, The Reliquary's Shrine of the Eternals has a decidedly anti-elitist slant to its election process in that the voting is done not by sportswriters but by ordinary fans, who are members of the organization. Each year three new inductees from a list of fifty candidates are elected, and the Shrine's roster so far is a diverse one indeed, including Moe Berg, Jim Bouton, Dock Ellis, Mark Fidrych, Curt Flood, Shoeless Joe Jackson, Bill Lee, Minnie Minoso, Satchel Paige, Jimmy Piersall, Pam Postema, and Bill Veeck.

As an institution, The Baseball Reliquary is in its infancy. The organization is still looking for a permanent home for its unusual collection of baseball artifacts; and its Induction Day Ceremonies, which are scheduled, and brazenly so some might say, on the same day each year as those of the National Baseball Hall of Fame, do not attract anywhere near the same attention as those in Cooperstown. Yet, don't bet against The Baseball Reliquary. It may be that the odds are greater that baseball fans will embrace this unique institution and the spirit behind it than an award given to Ty Cobb for his "humanitarianism" will be found—if it weren't for the fact that such an award is already part of The Baseball Reliquary's collection!

You may not have ever heard of Mark Hubbs of Dayton, Ohio, but he became quite a celebrity in Cincinnati on Opening Day of the 2003 season. Here's how.

To stir up a little extra interest for its annual Opening Day Parade through the streets of Cincinnati, the Findlay Market Association decided to sponsor a Pete Rose look-alike contest, with the winner receiving two tickets to the Opening Day game between the Reds and the Pittsburgh Pirates and a place of honor riding in the parade. Hubbs did not have tickets to the sold-out game, but when his daughter Melanie heard about the contest on the radio, she knew that, if she could talk her dad into entering the contest, then she and her dad were not going to have to watch the game on television. After all, people had been mistaking her dad, with his square jaw and flattop haircut, for Pete Rose for years.

Hubbs, who is nine months older than the real Pete, remembers the confusion starting in earnest as his body started filling out when he was about twenty-four years old. "One Sunday a little while after I'd gotten married," he says, "when my wife and I were sitting in church, some little boy sitting behind us kept telling his parents throughout the service that Pete Rose was sitting in front of them. Boy, was he disappointed afterward when I told him the truth. After that, the mistaken identity thing happened all the time. When Pete was chasing the Ty Cobb record, my wife and I couldn't go anywhere without people noticing us, which was kind of fun. But then when he got into all that trouble, I was kind of ashamed to be mistaken for him. So, it's been both a positive and a negative thing."

According to one of the organizers of the contest, Bob Pickford, "The whole thing was just a publicity stunt, something we thought would be good for a few laughs. For instance, we only had one rule: 'No pets, please.' But the thing gathered a momentum we hadn't expected. *USA Today* ran a little notice about the contest, and people started calling from out of town to ask whether or not they should fly in to participate in it." And they never expected to get an entry like Mark Hubbs, whose uncanny resemblance to Rose caused four of the sixteen entrants to immediately drop out of the competition at registration on Opening Day.

After being officially declared the winner of the contest, Hubbs stole the show while riding in the parade wearing a Reds cap and jacket. "I got more attention than the grand marshall of the parade, Tom Browning, who pitched a perfect game for the Reds," says Hubbs, "and a lot of people who didn't know about the contest thought I was really Pete Rose until somebody told them about the contest. Everybody was so friendly, I kept thinking, Where are all these nice people coming from? Riding in that parade, I didn't feel like I deserved the great way everybody was treating me." Later, at the Reds' new Great American Ballpark, Hubbs posed with fans for hundreds of photos and signed countless fake "Pete Rose"-over-Mark Hubbs autographs. The highlight of the day for Mark was getting to meet former Reds manager Sparky Anderson, and Hubbs is such a dead ringer for Rose that even Sparky was fooled for a few moments until after he'd given Rose's double a big enthusiastic hug.

And what was the reaction of Rose himself? Rose has met Hubbs only once, years ago. "Pete only had one thing to say," says Hubbs. "'I don't want you making any money off of me.' I was a little disappointed that he would say that, but I understood the way he felt."

One of baseball's most enduring myths is the "Curse of the Bambino": the notion that the failure of the Boston Red Sox to win the World Series since 1918 is due to the team's having sold Babe Ruth, the greatest player in baseball history, to the New York Yankees. While preposterous, the superstition has been popularized by a Dan Shaughnessy book and facetiously embraced by long-suffering Boston fans who find it to be a convenient explanation for an incredible run of heartbreaking near misses.

Red Sox fans have come up with all sorts of suggestions for ways of lifting the curse, such as having a priest perform an exorcism, making a penitential pilgrimage to Babe Ruth's birthplace at the Babe Ruth Museum in Baltimore, and maintaining an empty locker with the Babe's picture in it at Fenway Park, à la the Phantom of the Opera who wanted a seat reserved for him at the Paris Opera House.

Nothing's worked yet, and perhaps for that reason Red Sox fans seem to be carrying their efforts to new heights of ridiculousness. For instance, according to the *Boston Globe*, real estate investor Paul Giorgio carried his concerns about the dark cloud hanging over the Red Sox with him as he made an arduous ascent up Mount Everest. "At base camp, every team gets its gear blessed by the lama," said Giorgio, "so I asked the lama how I might break the Curse of the Bambino." On May 23, 2001, Giorgio reached the summit of Mount Everest, and, following the advice of the Tibetan holy man, planted a Red Sox ball cap on top of the world, right next to an American flag. Trained by his Red Sox experience to expect disaster at the moment of imminent victory, Giorgio felt the need to bolster the lama's strategy by burning a New York Yankees cap which he'd also carried with him to the top of Everest. Naturally, neither the lama's blessing nor Giorgio's symbolic gesture worked. After being in contention for most of the 2001 season, the Red Sox collapsed at the end of the season, losing twenty-six of thirty-eight before winning their last five meaningless games. As this book goes to press, the curse lives on!

THE FRONTIER LEAGUE

M inor league teams that are professional but not affiliated with major league organizations are called Independents. The 1990s witnessed a remarkable revival of Independent professional baseball, and one of the most successful of these ventures has been the Frontier League, which began play in 1993 with franchises in eight small towns in Ohio, Kentucky, and West Virginia. Heading into the 2003 season, only one of the original members was still alive, the Paints of Chillicothe, Ohio; yet the league itself was prospering, having expanded to twelve teams located in six Midwestern states.

It goes without saying that the early days in the Frontier League were a struggle. Kevin Rouch, current deputy commissioner of the league, relates an incident that provides an intimation of just how bad things were. "This was in 1995 when we had a team in Zanesville, Ohio, and I was the radio broadcaster for the team, called the Greys," says Rouch. "We made road trips in an old yellow school bus that the team had painted grey. It was a piece of junk with suspension so bad it was guaranteed to ruin your kidneys. One day we were on I-70 headed to a game in Johnstown, Pennsylvania, and the bus broke down. The bus driver pulled this old crate over onto the berm, and there we were, stuck in the middle of nowhere. Now, I was only thirty-five years old, but compared to the players on our team I was an old man, and so I always did whatever I could to curry favor with them in order to make my job a little easier. Well, I immediately recognized this as an opportunity to do just that.

"I had an early version of a cell phone with me, so I called information and got the number of a local pizza place. I ordered twenty pizzas and ten two-liter bottles of soda pop, and, believe it or not, they delivered to us on the side of the highway! Some of the guys climbed on top of the bus and ate their pizza up there, and that's actually how we got rescued. Some of the motorists passing by got concerned and called the emergency authorities, and they sent out some local cops who told the players to climb down because it wasn't safe to be up there on top of a disabled bus. The whole thing was a pain in the neck, but the upshot was that I was a hero with the team for the rest of the season!"

The Independent leagues were started with two purposes in mind. One was to bring professional baseball to cities and communities left out of the affiliated minor leagues system. The other was to provide playing opportunities for both players released by affiliated teams and players never signed by major league organizations in the first place. Whenever an Independent league player gets signed or re-signed by a major league organization and works his way up to the big leagues, everyone associated with that Independent league rejoices because the player's success validates their efforts and the whole concept of Independent league baseball. The Frontier League has sent a number of its graduates on to the major leagues, including San Diego Padres pitcher Brian Tolberg, St. Louis Cardinals pitcher Jason Simontacchi, and former Boston Red Sox first baseman/designated hitter Morgan Burkhart.

Even some of the Frontier League players who never made it fell short for reasons other than lack of talent. For example, the only thing that kept Frontier League legend Gator McBride of the Chillicothe Paints from eventually becoming a major league player was injuries. John Wend, who doubles as both Chillicothe's director of sales and marketing and the team's PA announcer in the press box, tells a story that illustrates just how good McBride was. "When the Atlanta Braves told us they were releasing Gator, they said, 'We will never send you a better hitter than this guy,' and that was the truth. The only reason they released him was that he kept having trouble with his hamstrings. If they had invested big bonus money in him, they'd never have let him go. They'd have babied him until he got healthy. He'd hit one off the wall in center field in Chillicothe and get a single because of his bad hamstring. Sometimes he'd have two bad hamstrings at the same time! Every time he'd hit a triple, we'd pray as he was running around the bases that he wouldn't pull up lame. It was a shame he couldn't overcome his injuries because Gator was a great hitter. In the only full season he played for us he hit .403 and lost the batting title by one point to Morgan Burkhart.

"Gator hardly ever struck out, and he never swung at bad pitches. The first and only time I saw him called out on strikes, he turned around and said something real quietly to the umpire. I'd never seen him do that before, either. He never said a word to the umpires. After the game I asked the home plate ump what Gator had said to him, and he told me that Gator said, 'Sir, I've never taken a third strike in my life.'

"'And you know what?' the umpire said. 'It wasn't a strike. It was outside.'"

Besides offering its fans a good brand of baseball at very affordable ticket prices, the Frontier League has always been peopled by its share of characters, none more interesting than Max McLeary, who umpires in the league despite having lost an eye in an accident. A one-eyed umpire sounds like a joke, and McLeary has certainly heard them all (and then some) about him and his brethren in blue having bad eyesight, like "Hey, ump, you're blind in one eye and can't see out of the other one!" Yet McLeary tries to use his handicap to his advantage by outworking, outpreparing, and outhustling everybody else, and he is actually regarded as one of the very best arbiters in the league. He also has a great sense of humor and loves to tell stories about his glass eye that show he doesn't take himself and his unique predicament too seriously. His best story is the one called "The Mask Story."

"My first year in the league I was umpiring in Chillicothe on the next-to-the-last night of the season," says Max, "and one of my buddies, a guy named Bob Hughes, had come along to the game with me. The visiting team was batting in the fifth inning when the batter fouled one back. The catcher didn't even get his glove on the ball, and it came straight back, and went through the bars of my mask!

"The ball actually got stuck in my mask. And I mean it was stuck! Nobody could pull the ball out of my mask with his hands, and it took two of the strongest players on the Paints to hammer the ball loose with a bat. We figured out later that the ball had to have been tipped perfectly with the bat and that it had to have hit the mask dead-on perfectly. It was just a freak accident.

"Of course, when the ball went through my mask, it hit me in the face. I went down like I'd been shot. My nose was broken, there was blood all over my face, and I had a concussion. I remember the Chillicothe catcher standing over me, saying,

'Max is bleeding!' He was saying that to the Paints' trainer and the team doctor, who were rushing onto the field. Then I passed out.

"My buddy Bob Hughes was coming back from the concession stands when this happened. At first he thought the batter had gotten plunked, but then he realized that it was me on the ground being attended to. The medical people were really worried. They didn't think I was going to make it there for a while. There's no trauma center out there in Ross County, so they called Columbus, the state capitol about an hour north of Chillicothe, and had an emergency helicopter on standby.

"The trainer, who didn't know me real well yet, took out one of those small flashlights, and when he shined it in my eye, he didn't get the reaction he was looking for. He said, 'We're losing him! His eye is glassing over!'

"And Bob Hughes, who's standing behind the backstop with a Pepsi in one hand and a bag of popcorn in the other, shouts, *'Check his other eye!'*"

Finally, here's a story about a nightmare rookie debut, as told by Chillicothe Paints All-Star outfielder Matt McCay, who went into the Frontier League after an outstanding college career at North Carolina Wesleyan College and the University of North Carolina. "I had a terrible tryout with the Paints, but they signed me anyway," McCay says, "mainly, I think, because I'd told them I could also catch, and they figured that my versatility would come in handy. A week into the season I started at catcher against the Dubois County Dragons in the first professional game I ever played in.

"Everything was fine until the top of the second when Dragons outfielder Scott Marple came up to bat with two outs. I put down a one for the fastball, but Ryan Lardi, our pitcher, shook me off. So I put two fingers down for the curve. He shook me off again. After I put down three for the change-up and got shook off a third time, I just held my glove up as if to say, 'Okay. Throw whatever you want.' Because Lardi didn't have any other pitches. The pitch came in, and it was a fastball right at Marple, who hit the dirt to get out of the way. I threw the ball back to Lardi, he shook me off again three times, and then he threw another knock-down pitch. Now, it was obvious that Lardi was trying to hit Marple, who was swearing and cussing at Lardi and really getting angry. I told him, 'Hey, man, I'm just a rookie in this league. I'm not calling those pitches.' The first two pitches were up around Marple's shoulders. Lardi's third pitch was around the knees, but it, too, was way inside and almost hit Marple. This time Marple took a step or two forward as if he were thinking about charging the mound, so I told him, 'Look, I don't know what's going on between you two, but if you head for the mound, I'm going to have to stop you.'

"I thought maybe Lardi would finally start pitching to Marple, but no—the fourth pitch was the worst of all. It was two feet above and two feet behind Marple's head. I jumped up and ran out in front of the plate to intercept Marple, but he'd already started toward first, mouthing off against Lardi all the way, because the pitch was ball four. I started hollering at Lardi, 'Man, what are you doing?' but he only held up his glove to ask me for the ball so he could get ready for the next batter. I turned around to ask the umpire for a new ball, but he gave me a disgusted look and motioned backward with his thumb. Then I realized with horror that the ball was in play back at the backstop and that Marple was starting to run around the bases! By the time I picked up the ball I thought I had a play on

Marple at third, but my throw short-hopped our third baseman. It got past him, and Marple came in to score.

"'Oh, my gosh,' I thought, 'this is my first pro game, and I've just given up an inside-the-park base on balls.' Our manager, Roger Hanners, came out of the dugout and said, 'Son, what just happened?'

"I tried to explain that, yes, I'd forgotten that Lardi's last pitch to Marple was still in play, but that was because I was concerned about protecting my pitcher. Roger said, 'Okay. Could have happened to anybody. There's two outs. Try to remember that, will you?'"

PHIL GARNER

Major league teams don't have to function as twenty-four-hour mutual-admiration societies in order to be successful, as long as the players can leave their personal differences and petty grievances behind in the clubhouse. The powerhouse Oakland A's of the early 1970s were able to do that. And so were the World Champion 1979 Pittsburgh Pirates, who, according to Pirates pitcher Kent Tekulve, were "the United Nations of Baseball. We fought like cats and dogs before the game. Then we'd come together, go out, and play winning baseball. After the game, we'd fight like cats and dogs again.

"The two main instigators in the clubhouse were Phil Garner and Dave Parker. Garner was a second baseman we'd gotten from Oakland, and his nickname was 'Scrap Iron' because he was so tough. He'd scratch, claw, bite—do whatever he needed to do to help us win. And Parker was a big, strong guy with a loud voice. But he didn't intimidate Garner, and the two of them went at it almost every day. The clubhouse would be quiet as long as only one of them was in it, but, as soon as the other one came in, all hell would break loose. Garner would say something like, 'You can't hit, you big donkey.' And then Parker would say, 'I guarantee you three things are gonna happen today: the sun is gonna come up, the sun is gonna go down, and I'm gonna get at least two base knocks in this game.'

"Verbally, Garner and Parker probably ended the season in a tie, but I'd have to say that Phil got the best of Dave in the end because of one gag he pulled at Dave's expense. As you may remember, Parker had this funny, sort of disdainful way of catching fly balls, whereby he would snatch the ball out of the air with a real sharp downward motion. Well, one day he caught a fly ball like that, and the ball slipped out of his glove when he jerked it downward. It was an error, but we didn't give a crap because it didn't hurt us, and we won the game.

"The next day when we went out on the field to start loosening up for batting practice, Garner said, 'Teke, get some balls and come on out here.' While I gathered up some baseballs, Garner put on Parker's jersey and taped around his waist one of those big white pickle buckets we use to hold baseballs. He went out into the infield and had me loft baseballs, one at a time, up into the air. He would zigzag around with his arms stretched out to his sides like he was disoriented, and then at the last second he'd catch the ball in the bucket around his waist. Of course the ball bounced way out of the bucket every time. And the whole time we were doing this, he was saying, 'Who am I? Who am I?'"

GNOMES

In the summer of 2001 a mysterious crime wave struck fear into the hearts of gardeners in Newark, New York, a tiny rural village twenty-five miles west of Rochester. Miniature elves, animals, mythical creatures, and figurines of all sorts were being abducted from Newark flower beds and in their places were left the calling cards of a group identifying itself as the "Garden Gnome Liberation Front."

The case baffled Newark police, and in early August things took an even stranger turn. Investigating a report of trespassing at a local ballpark, officers arrived at the scene to find twenty-four plastic, concrete, and ceramic figurines strategically placed around the diamond as if they were playing a baseball game. The officers attempted to check in with HQ, but as officer Tim Vanderline says, "We were laughing too hard to say anything." The police broke up the game but made no arrests.

Everyone was not so amused by the gnome-napping, especially seventy-four-year-old victim Jessie Rice, who said, "I don't think it's funny. Stealing is stealing." Five of Rice's ten pilfered gnomes were found at the baseball game and returned to her by police. Unfortunately, two of them, a doe and a yard mushroom, came back damaged and were placed on Rice's Garden DL. A few days later Rice received a bouquet of yellow daisies and a note that said, "With our sincere apology for the broken gnomes—GGLF." In response to the gesture Rice said, "I appreciated the flowers, but I wish they realized that they hurt people when they steal. I am going to try to fix my mushroom. I loved that one."

THE HALL OF FAME

When a player learns that he has been elected to the National Baseball Hall of Fame, he is usually ecstatic, humbled, and awed all at the same time. After all, he realizes in a flash that his achievements on the diamond are now going to be immortalized and represented by a bronze plaque of his likeness that will hang forever, along with those of his peers, in the Hall of Fame Gallery. The plaques are thus serious business, and the Hall of Fame oversees all aspects of their creation, such as their wording and sculpting. However, whenever a player spent significant portions of his career with more than one team, the decision about which team's cap and uniform to use on the plaque is left up to the player. And, as several recent inductees have discovered, it can be an excruciating decision to make. Catcher Carlton Fisk, for instance, who actually spent most of his career with the Chicago White Sox, agonized over the matter until he finally decided that he wanted to be depicted on his plaque wearing the uniform of the Boston Red Sox, the team he played for first. Pitcher Catfish Hunter never could decide between the Kansas City/Oakland A's and the New York Yankees, and so he settled for the compromise of a plaque that shows him wearing a plain, letterless cap.

When outfielder Dave Winfield was elected to the Hall of Fame in 2001, he was faced with the same dilemma as Fisk and Hunter. Although Winfield played for six different teams during his twenty-two-year career, everyone knew that his decision was going to come down to two teams, the San Diego Padres (the team Winfield had begun his major league career with) and the New York Yankees. The Yankees seemed to have the edge in that Winfield was proud to have worn the fabled pinstripes of Ruth and Gehrig. On the other hand, there were still some hard feelings between Winfield and Yankees owner George Steinbrenner, who saddled Winfield with the insulting nickname "Mr. May" for Winfield's inability to perform as well in the post-season as Reggie Jackson, "Mr. October."

In Cooperstown on Induction Sunday it was New York governor George Pataki who informed the masses of Winfield's decision in a most witty way. In what was basically a "Welcome to New York" speech, Pataki congratulated each new inductee. When it came time to talk about Winfield, Pataki introduced him in seemingly sacrilegious terms that momentarily shocked the heavily pro-Yankees crowd.

"And now, I welcome Dave Winfield, the greatest Yankee to enter the Hall of Fame . . . [*gasp!*] as a Padre!" he said.

E verybody knows about the true baseball immortals such as Babe Ruth, Ty Cobb, and Joe DiMaggio, but what about Cooperstown's lesser greats, the players we might call paradoxically "the obscure Hall of Famers"? As strange as it sounds, there are a number of players in the Hall of Fame who are not famous at all, judging by the average fan's familiarity with their lives and careers. Chief among these is George Stacey Davis, the "dead-ball era's" best-hitting shortstop and a player most fans had not even heard of until he was voted into the Hall of Fame in 1998 by the Veterans Committee, almost ninety years after he retired from the game.

The exploits of George Davis, like those of all but the most sensational of nineteenth-century players, have been long forgotten by everyone except for the most diligent students of the period. What makes Davis a special case, though, is that he has been a mystery even to the baseball scholars who are dedicated to the nineteenth century. Realizing that Davis had dropped completely out of sight around 1920, former Hall of Fame librarian and pioneer baseball researcher Lee Allen spent many years in the 1960s trying to track Davis down, in order to fill out his post-baseball biography. Allen discovered little besides the fact that Davis died in a Philadelphia hospital on October 17, 1940, was laid to rest in a pine box, and was buried in an unmarked grave. The most salient nonbaseball fact we know about Davis is that he and a couple of teammates dramatically rescued some women and children from a burning building they were passing on their way to the ballpark on April 26, 1900.

Although Davis never received a single vote from the sportswriters who take first crack at voting for the Hall of Fame, his credentials seemed impeccable once the Veterans Committee decided he was Hall of Fame material. He averaged over .300 for a nine-year stretch (1893–1901) with the New York Giants, led the National League in RBI in 1897 with 136 and knocked in 90 or more runs six times, had the highest fielding percentage in the league among shortstops four times, and finished his career with 2,665 hits and a .295 batting average. A member of the Chicago White Sox "Hitless Wonders" team that won the third World Series in 1906, Davis also became embroiled in the war between the National and American Leagues at the turn of the century. He jumped from the penurious Giants to the upstart and better-paying Chicago White Sox in 1902 but then wanted to return to the National League in 1903 when the Giants offered to make him the second-highest-paid player in the game, behind Napoleon Lajoie. Shortly thereafter, the two leagues made peace, and Davis was ordered to remain with the White Sox. This he eventually did, and for the remainder of his career, but only after some ineffectual attempts to disregard the order.

According to Lee Allen, "The Davis case was as famous in its day as the Sisler case, Scott Perry case, and Feller case of later eras. It almost wrecked the precarious peace made by the two majors in 1903."

George Davis was born in 1870 in Cohoes, New York, a town of 17,000 on the Hudson River just north of Albany. A busload of Cohoes residents made the trip to Cooperstown for Davis's induction into the National Baseball Hall of Fame in the summer of 1998. They were proud of their native son, but none of them were even distantly related to Davis. Thus, when it came time to induct him and accept the bronze plaque on his behalf, the honor fell to National League president Leonard Coleman, who said: "As evidenced by the fact that I'm accepting this award for him, no family member could be located. So in a way, baseball was—and is—George Davis's family. And as George sits resting with the Father, we hope that he will feel a great sense of pride that his family has granted him the highest distinction."

CHUCK HARMON

Chuck Harmon, a utility infielder who played for the Reds, Cardinals, and Phillies, became the first African-American to play for the Cincinnati Reds when he made his major league debut in 1953. As all African-Americans did in those days, Harmon experienced racial prejudice during his professional baseball career, but he never let it get him down or sour his views on life. Take, for example, Harmon's version of an incident that wasn't funny at all on the surface.

"One day in July of 1955, Jim Hearn of the New York Giants was pitching a no-hitter against us at the Polo Grounds," says Harmon, "and our manager Birdie Tebbets sent me up to pinch-hit with one out in the bottom of the ninth. I hit a dying quail over the head of shortstop Alvin Dark to break up Hearn's no-hitter, and my hit was the only one we got in the game. A couple of days later when we got home I got a letter in the mail from a Giants fan who didn't like the fact that it was me who'd gotten the hit that broke up Hearn's no-hitter. The guy said he was going to shoot me when we went back to New York to play if I walked on the field.

"Well, I turned the letter over to club officials, who turned it over to the FBI, and when we went into the Polo Grounds a couple of weeks later to play the Giants, there were some FBI agents there on assignment. The clubhouses were in center field in the Polo Grounds, and when it was time for us to go out on the field to work out before the game, I walked down the steps between the bleachers with Wally Post and Gus Bell. We got to the field and started walking in toward the infield when Post and Bell stopped and said, 'Oh, man—what in the hell are we doing? Chuck's supposed to get shot today!' So they both veered off and moved about twenty feet away from me. But they were only kidding, and they came back over to me and walked the rest of the way in right next to me, which I appreciated.

"Nothing happened, of course, but later people heard about the letter. They'd always ask me if I was scared, and I'd tell 'em, 'No, not really'. I figured if the guy who'd sent me the letter was a true New York fan, he wouldn't dare shoot me. Because if he did, our manager Birdie Tebbets would put a guy in the lineup who could really hit, and that would hurt the Giants worse than I did!"

Speaking of Reds manager Birdie Tebbets, Harmon remembers another incident that had an ugly beginning but a humorous ending. "We always had tough battles with the St. Louis Cardinals," says Chuck, "and one day when we were playing them, Birdie and the Cardinals' manager Harry 'The Hat' Walker were really going at it, jawing back and forth from the dugouts. The arguing escalated until somebody got hit with a pitch, which caused the umpire to call both of them up to home plate. When they got up to the plate, they were still jawing and cussing at each other. One of them grabbed the other one, and the other one grabbed him back. One of them pushed the other one, and then the other one pushed him back. Before you knew it, they fell to the ground and started wrestling. While they were on the ground rolling around, their caps came off. The umps were able to stop them after a minute or so and get them separated. They stood up, put their caps back on, and started walking back to the dugouts, but then everybody started hollering at them and laughing at the same time. When they stopped and looked at each other, Birdie could see that Walker was wearing his cap, and Walker could see that Birdie was wearing his. Then they started laughing about it, too. They walked up, swapped hats, and hugged each other. And, I guess because they made up so nicely, the ump didn't throw either one of them out of the game."

CHRIS HOOK

When a minor league player becomes a major leaguer, he joins an exclusive fraternity that he will belong to for the rest of his life. No matter how his life and career turn out afterward, anybody who makes it to the big leagues will always be accorded a certain, almost palpable, respect by his fellow major leaguers that others can do nothing to earn. In addition, to gain the complete respect and acceptance of one's teammates, a player has to make a meaningful contribution to the success of the team. When a player feels that he truly belongs, when he knows that his teammates completely accept him as an equal—that, too, is a special moment in any player's career.

Former San Francisco Giants relief pitcher Chris Hook remembers reaching that point in his career as a rookie in 1995. It came when Hook and the Giants were making their first trip of the season into Los Angeles to face the Giants' long-standing rivals, the despised Dodgers. Mike Krukow, one of the Giants' broadcasters and a former Giants pitcher himself, came up to Chris before the first game of the series and said, "Psst! Chris, come here. You are becoming an important part of the team and, before you go into battle against the Dodgers, whom we hate, as you know, I want to share something with you that we reveal only to the guys we feel are true Giants." And that said, Krukow showed Hook the secret Giants handshake.

That was the moment when Chris Hook knew that he had truly arrived as a major league player.

When I asked Hook if he could show me, a lifelong Giants fan, the secret handshake, he said, "I could. But then I'd have to kill you."

CHARLIE HOUGH

The first All-Star Game I covered as a writer was the fifty-seventh, which took place July 15, 1986, in the Astrodome in Houston, Texas. The game was dominated by pitching, by the likes of twenty-one-year-old rookie Roger Clemens (the game's MVP) and Fernando Valenzuela (who struck out five American League batters in a row). But for me the most memorable stint on the hill was turned in by a thirty-eight-year-old knuckleballer named Charlie Hough, who almost lost the game for the American League.

Hough had broken in with the Dodgers back in 1970, and prior to his appearance in the 1986 All-Star Game, he was best known for having been the third of three Los Angeles pitchers who were victimized by Reggie Jackson's three consecutive first-pitch home runs in Game Six of the 1977 World Series. Charlie spent a decade working out of the Los Angeles bullpen, but the Texas Rangers, to whom he was traded during the 1980 season, made him a starter. He became the workhorse of their staff, racking up more than two hundred innings pitched eight times in a nine-year period.

Appearing in his first All-Star Game, Hough was the third pitcher to take the mound for the American League, and he started the bottom of the seventh with his team holding a 3–0 edge on the Nationals. Now, maybe American League manager Dick Howser figured that Hough's knuckleball would stymie the National Leaguers after they'd spent the first six innings trying unsuccessfully to catch up with the heat thrown by Clemens and Milwaukee's Teddy Higuera. Maybe he had a sentimental streak and wanted to reward Charlie for all the hard work he'd put in over the years. Or maybe he just didn't feel comfortable going to some of the other pitchers down in the American League All-Stars bullpen—guys like Cleveland's Ken Schrom, California's Mike Witt, and Detroit's Willie Hernandez. I'm not sure what Howser's reasoning was, but I do remember thinking that Dick was asking for trouble by sending an old fart with a trick pitch into a pressure-packed situation to do battle against the best hitters in the National League.

Although the seventh inning went smoothly for Hough, three up and three down, the eighth was a different story. Chris Brown of the Giants led off with a double to deep left-center. Charlie struck out Chili Davis, but the third strike, a knuckleball, got away from catcher Rich Gedman for a wild pitch. Brown advanced to third when Gedman had to throw to first to retire Davis. Charlie then struck out Montreal Expo Hubie Brooks, but the third strike again got away from Gedman. This time the ruling was a passed ball. Brooks reached first safely, and Brown slid home, under the late tag of Hough, with the National League's first run of the game. After balking Brooks to second, Hough whiffed Montreal's Tim Raines on a knuckler that Gedman was able to hang on to. When Charlie gave up another hit, a single to Dodger Steve Sax, which drove in Brooks from second, Howser finally decided he'd seen enough. Dave Righetti came on to relieve Hough, who left having struck out three batters in the inning. Righetti ended the inning when he got Houston's Glen Davis to pop out to third. The two runs given up by Hough set the stage for a tense ending to the game. In the bottom of the ninth the National League put runners on first and second with one out, but Don Aase replaced Righetti and was able to preserve the 3–2 victory for the American League by getting Chris Brown to ground into a game-ending double play.

After the game the slightly peeved Gedman, who'd never caught a knuckleballer before, said, "That was embarrassing." At least that was all he said that was fit for us to print.

As for Charlie, he never made the All-Star Team again, but he kept right on playing, almost for another decade. From Texas he went to the White Sox for a couple of seasons and then to the expansion Florida Marlins for a couple of more. He threw the first pitch in Marlins history on Opening Day in 1993, against his original team, the Dodgers. He might have kept on throwing the knuckleball in the major leagues for several more years had he not required surgery for a bad hip the following winter. He retired after a twenty-five-year major league career "even-Steven"—with a record of 216–216.

MAGIC JOHNSON

As one of the all-time greats of the National Basketball Association, former Los Angeles Laker Earvin "Magic" Johnson has a lot of money to invest. One of the things he did with his moola was to buy partial ownership of a minor league baseball team, the Dayton Dragons of the Midwest League. Naturally, Magic was one of the first celebrities selected to throw out a ceremonial first pitch at a Dragons game during the team's inaugural season in 2000.

According to Dragons director of media relations and broadcasting Mike Vander Wood, Magic's first pitch performance was one to remember. "He made a terrible throw," says Mike. "It bounced two or three times before it got to the catcher. But somebody had a basketball in the dugout—I guess the person had brought it to get Magic to autograph it—and when the person with the basketball saw Magic have trouble with the baseball, he rolled the basketball out to the mound. Magic picked up the basketball, climbed back onto the pitching rubber, and went into a whole pitching routine. While holding the basketball in one hand, he lifted his arms over his head, brought them down into a stretch position at his belt, looked back at second to check the runner, lifted his leg, and then fired a strike, a real bullet, all the way to the catcher. Nearly knocked him over with it. The crowd went nuts!

"Afterward, I interviewed Magic in the radio booth. I asked him if he had been as good a baseball player in high school as he had been a basketball player. He said, 'Nah, baseball was never my game. When I pitched, that's exactly how the ball looked coming into the batter—as big as a basketball!' "

AL KALINE

Leon Roberts, a tremendous high school athlete and a two-sport All-American as a Michigan prepster, made the majors as an outfielder and played with five different clubs over an eleven-year career. His best season came in 1978 with the Seattle Mariners, when he hit .301 with 22 home runs and 78 RBI. Roberts appeared in only seventeen games with Detroit as a rookie in 1974, but he was there to witness a historic moment in the career of Tigers great Al Kaline, as well as the backdrop to it, which escaped the attention of everybody else.

"Even though I was just a rookie, they lockered me right next to Kaline," says Roberts. "Al was as nice as they come, a real class guy, and he was also kind of quiet. He didn't say much to me. He'd talk to me if I asked him about something, but he sort of let me alone otherwise to watch and learn and figure things out for myself. One time, though, I guess he felt he had to say something. I hadn't even been up for one week—not one week—when this happened. We were losing by a bunch of runs but made a big comeback in the bottom of the eighth inning. We rallied and rallied and rallied and finally went ahead. After somebody hit an infield pop-up, I thought, 'All we have to do is get three outs, and we win the game.' I was in the lineup that day, and I was so pumped up I led the charge out of the dugout: 'Let's go get 'em, boys!' I ran all the way out to the third baseline with my glove before I realized that nobody had followed me out of the dugout. I made a U-turn and jogged back in. When I sat down next to Al he said, 'Hey, rook, we

get three outs every inning in this league these days.' I was so embarrassed I wanted to crawl under the bench and hide.

"It was around this time that Kaline was closing in on three thousand hits, which was really a big deal back then. Pee Wee Reese, who worked as a sales rep for Hillerich & Bradsby, the bat company, came into our clubhouse after a game and said, 'Al, you've had a contract with us for a long time. Now that you're fixing to get your three thousandth hit, we'd really appreciate it if you'd use a Louisville Slugger when you get the big hit.'

"Kaline said, 'I am using a Louisville Slugger, Pee Wee.'

"And Pee Wee said, 'Well, I thought I saw you using an Adirondack bat today.'

" 'No, no,' said Al. See, back in those days the clubhouse guys used to keep all the bats together in a grocery shopping cart, so they could wheel the cart back and forth between the clubhouse and the dugout. What Al did was put a piece of slick, black electrician's tape on his bat below the trademark so he could easily pick it out of the shopping cart. Even though it wasn't his intention, the tape made Kaline's bat look from a distance like an Adirondack bat because all Adirondack bats came from the factory with a ring painted on them around the same place as where Al had put the tape on his bat. Al explained this to Pee Wee and implied that he didn't think it was a big deal.

"A few days later, after Kaline was even closer to three thousand hits, Pee Wee tried again: 'Al, we'd really appreciate it if you'd take the tape off your bat.'

" 'Okay, okay! I'll do it,' Kaline snapped.

"A few days later we were in Baltimore, and Kaline hit a duck fart off Dave McNally for his three thousandth hit. The sportswriters crowded around his locker after the game, but when they left Pee Wee came over and handed him a congratulatory check for three thousand dollars. 'That's why I wanted you to use our bat, Al,' he said.

"And Kaline, who'd been immediately sorry for snapping at Pee Wee, because normally Kaline never said a harsh word to anyone, really felt bad about it then."

KIDS

For years, Hall of Fame induction ceremonies took place on the steps of the National Baseball Library in downtown Cooperstown, New York. When the lawn in front of the library could no longer hold the ever-growing crowds of fans, the ceremonies were moved to the grounds of the Clark Sports Center, just south of downtown Cooperstown. Every summer since, during the weekend when the newest Hall of Famers are inducted, enterprising Cooperstown youngsters set up lemonade stands on every corner of town, or so it seems. It takes a little effort in such a competitive environment to make one's refreshment business stand out from all the others, but ten-year-old Nicholas Voreyer of 94 Pioneer Street found a way to do just that in the summer of 2002, when Ozzie Smith headlined the incoming class of baseball immortals.

Fans who made the short walk from downtown Cooperstown to the Clark Sports Center by passing down Pioneer Street on Sunday, July 28, were no doubt impressed by the marketing savvy of Master Voreyer. The poster sign at the stand, run by Nicholas, his brother Thomas (aged eight), neighbors Henry Bauer (ten), Benny Bauer (eight), and Erin Henrici (nine), did more than simply list the prices being charged for lemonade, cookies, and brownies. Thanks to Nicholas, under the heading "Facts About Ozzie Smith," it provided the following key information that any baseball fan would be delighted to have:

- Ozzie Smith played for the Cardinals and Padres.
- Ozzie Smith played shortstop.
- Ozzie Smith's number was 1 on both teams.

When asked why he had decided to use such a tactic as a means of attracting business to the stand, Nicholas said, "I knew Ozzie Smith was going into the Hall of Fame, and I thought that people would like to read it."

In addition to performing a valuable public educational service, the Pioneer Street Lemonaders did a brisk business on the day, taking in $32.50, which was split five ways. "We also had to eat some leftovers," said Nicholas, who himself consumed five cookies, two brownies, and five glasses of lemonade to aid the cause.

A s the popular 1960s Art Linkletter television show proved for many years, "kids say the darndest things!" Here's a baseball story that makes the same point, as told by Jerry Hazelbaker, a world class musician and songwriter who admired George Brett so much that he named his second son after the Kansas City Royals' third baseman.

"In 1993 a guy from our neighborhood, Tommy Kramer, was a rookie with the Cleveland Indians," says Hazelbaker. "I'm great friends with Tommy today, but at the time I didn't know him as well as I do now. Nevertheless, when we decided we wanted to go up to Cleveland from Cincinnati to watch Tommy pitch, he couldn't have been nicer.

"In Tommy's previous start he had pitched a fantastic game— almost a perfect game! He gave up only one hit, a home run to Julio Franco, and Texas got no other base runners in the game. We were going to watch Tommy pitch against the Royals, and I took my eight-year-old son, George Brett Hazelbaker, along so he could see his namesake play.

"As I said, Tommy Kramer couldn't have been nicer. Instead of just leaving tickets for us at the ballpark's Will Call window, he had us come over to his apartment in Strongsville, Ohio, so we could all ride into Cleveland together. As we were walking out the door of his apartment, Tommy's wife hollered at him, 'Don't forget to take out the garbage.' I thought, 'Wow! Major leaguers still have to take out the garbage!'

"I was really looking forward to seeing Tommy pitch, but George was excited about getting to watch George Brett play. On the way to Municipal Stadium he asked Tommy if he would give Brett some good pitches to hit.

"I was hoping that George might actually get to meet George Brett with Tommy's help, and I brought my camera along just in case. However, Tommy said that because he was pitching, it would probably be easier for him to introduce George to George Brett the following day instead, so I left my camera in the car. Tommy took George into the clubhouse to meet some of the Indians' players, while I relaxed in the empty grandstands. After a while, the Royals came out on the field and started loosening up and stretching. Tommy and George came out of the Indians' dugout, and Tommy told me later that he saw Brett and figured, 'What the heck. Now's as good a time as any.'

"Tommy went up to Brett and said, 'Excuse me, Mr. Brett—you don't know who I am, but my name is Tom Kramer.'

"Brett said, 'I know who you are. You're that kid who almost pitched a perfect game against Texas! What can I do for you?'

"Tommy said, 'Well, one of my friends thinks so much of you that he named his son after you. This is George Brett Hazelbaker, and he'd like to meet you.'

"I'll never forget what happened next. Brett got a big smile on his face, he tousled the hair on George's head, and then he picked him off the ground and gave him a big bear hug! And I was so disappointed that I'd left my camera in the car.

"When Brett put George Brett down he asked him, 'What can I do for you tonight, George?'

"George said, 'Can you hit a home run off Tommy?'

"Tommy and Brett both laughed. Then Brett said, 'That's up to your buddy.'

"Tommy said, 'Every time you come up to bat tonight the first pitch will be a fastball down the middle.'

"Tommy did exactly what he said he was going to do, but Brett didn't hit a home run against him. Tommy pitched well but got relieved late in the game, and he got a no-decision. The great thing is that Brett did hit a home run, against an Indians reliever named Jeremy Hernandez. So, the game turned out great. I got to see Tommy pitch a whale of a game, and George got to see his namesake hit a home run—one that, thankfully, didn't come against Tommy."

TED KLUSZEWSKI

Until Johnny Bench and George Foster came along, Ted Kluszewski was the greatest slugger in the history of the Cincinnati Reds. The extremely popular first baseman was a naturally powerful physical specimen in the days before athletes bulked up in the weight room, and he had biceps so big he cut off the sleeves of his uniform shirt to accommodate them. In imitation of Big Klu, the Reds cut the sleeves off the shirts of all their players, thus giving birth to the sleeveless vest style of jersey that became the team's trademark for more than a decade.

Despite his intimidating size and strength, Kluszewski was a gentle giant without any pretentiousness, as the following story illustrates.

Late in the 1956 season Kluszewski suffered a slipped disc in his back, and he was bothered by the injury the rest of his career. In the following off-season, he decided to improve his home with a room addition onto the back of his house. When the workers arrived and began digging the footings in the backyard, Ted went outside to join them. The workers were thrilled to have a major league baseball star like Kluszewski shoot the breeze with them, but Ted's wife, Eleanor, viewed the situation differently.

When she spied Big Klu, arms folded across his chest, standing idly above ground, watching the hired help work, she stepped outside the house and shouted, "Theodore! Don't just stand there watching. Get down there and help those men dig!"

Grabbing a shovel, Kluszewski instantly did as he was told. As he did, his wife added, "You know you've got a bad back. The exercise will do you good."

TOMMY LASORDA

Todd Benzinger, a switch-hitting first baseman who played with five major league teams, didn't grow up a Tommy Lasorda fan, but he became a convert after he was traded to the Los Angeles Dodgers from the Kansas City Royals.

"Getting traded to the Dodgers was the best thing that ever happened to me," says Benzinger. "I was really happy to be going to Los Angeles because they had a great team there, and the Dodgers always do things first class. But I've always been a person who says what he's thinking. When I got traded, a reporter from Cincinnati, where I'd played a couple of years, wanted to know how I felt about the Dodgers. Well, I'd grown up right outside Cincinnati, and like all Reds fans I hated the Dodgers. I said that, and I also told the guy that I thought Lasorda was a big phony and that all that stuff about him 'bleeding Dodger Blue' was a bunch of crap.

"My comments were published in *USA Today*, which everybody in baseball reads, and right before I went out to Los Angeles to attend a press conference officially announcing the trade, my agent called and said, 'Look, Todd, I know you were just telling the truth, but you've got to apologize to Lasorda. You don't want to get off on the wrong foot.'

"When I met Tommy I did apologize, and he said, 'Todd, don't worry about it. Nobody cares about that stuff. You're a Dodger now, and you're gonna be great.' I immediately liked the guy and found out that he really is sincere.

"I also found out that he is quite a character. At the time Tommy was a spokesman for the diet drink called Slim Fast.

He had cases of it in his office, and he was always drinking it and trying to give cans of it to everybody else. But Tommy also ate whatever he wanted to, and he loved to eat. The players always have a couple of long tables of food set out for them after games, which we call 'the spread.' Well, Tommy always had his own spread in his office, before and after the games. One time I was the last player to leave the locker room. I wasn't in the starting lineup, but I wanted to be on the bench for the start of the game. I walked past the manager's office about three minutes before the game started, and Tommy was in there, eating. He said, 'Todd, Todd, come in here. Taste this pasta. A friend just brought it over.' He fixed me a big plate of it and said, 'It's great, isn't it?' I couldn't believe it. There I was, pigging out, with the manager of the ball club, in his office, right as the game was getting started.

"Tommy really knew his baseball, but when I joined the team he was getting to the age where he wasn't as much of a hands-on manager as he had been before. I didn't start a lot that year unless Eric Davis or Darryl Strawberry got hurt, so I was mostly coming off the bench. One night at Dodger Stadium it was early in the game, and Dave Anderson, Mike Piazza, who'd just been called up from the minors, and I were sitting on the bench next to Tommy. He was telling us stories about his playing career when he was with the Brooklyn Dodgers, and they were great stories too: 'I faced Stan Musial one day—blah, blah, blah.'

"Right in the middle of one of his stories there was a close play at first base, and it went against the Dodgers. We learned later that first baseman Eric Karros had had to stretch for a throw, and the ump called the runner safe. He said that Eric's foot had come off the bag. Karros was going crazy. When we realized that a brouhaha was starting, Tommy jumped up, looked all around, and went, 'Huh? Huh? What the hell is going on?'

"Even though he didn't have a clue about what had just happened, he ran out onto the field like a mad bull. He started arguing with the umpire, kicked dirt all over the place, and got tossed out of the game. Anderson, Piazza, and I all looked at each other in disbelief. We said, 'He didn't even see that play, did he?'

" 'Nope. Got kicked out of the game for a play he didn't even see!' "

LOUISVILLE SLUGGER

Bill Williams, vice president of public relations for the Hillerich & Bradsby Company, says that he has the easiest PR job in the world. "Publicity for our product, the Louisville Slugger bat, generates itself," he says. "The name Louisville Slugger is recognized by 87 percent of Americans, which puts it right up there with the country's most famous brands, such as Coca-Cola and Harley-Davidson, in terms of its 'unaided recall' quotient. Our bats are a nonthreatening icon for which people have an enormous affection. I've learned over the years when I'm traveling not to let other men I meet know that I work for Louisville Slugger. If I do, they are sure to tell me tearful stories about their first Louisville Slugger, which invariably their dads gave them. It's amazing. And if I have to carry a bat or two with me, everybody always wants to hold one and take a few practice cuts with it."

The allure of the Louisville Slugger is not hard to figure out. After all, the company dates back to 1884 when John A. "Bud" Hillerich turned a wooden bat for Pete "The Old Gladiator" Browning, who played for the Louisville Eclipse baseball team of the American Association. A decade later the name "Louisville Slugger" was registered with the United States Government as an official trademark. Early in the twentieth century Honus Wagner, Napoleon Lajoie, and Ty Cobb became the first players to sign promotional contracts with the company, and since then more than six thousand additional players have signed on with Louisville Slugger. One of the most fascinating exhibits at the Louisville Slugger Museum in downtown Louisville is the Signature Wall, which displays the signatures of the more than six thousand players burned into rectangular segments of bat barrel made of white ash wood. Baseball has changed a lot over the years, and other manufacturers have continually tried to gain a foothold in the bat business, but Louisville Slugger has remained a constant, reassuring part of the game—as well as the most famous bat in the world.

The best endorsements for Louisville Slugger bats have come from the players themselves, and nobody appreciated Louisville Sluggers more than Ted Williams—who was famous for visiting the factory, picking out the wood to be used for his bats himself, and handsomely tipping the factory workers in thanks for making his bats to his exact specifications. Williams once said, "I knew I'd arrived in the major leagues when I saw my name on a Louisville Slugger bat," and in 1993 he told Bill Williams in a letter that "I'd have been a .290 hitter without a Louisville Slugger."

Hall of Famer Joe Sewell, famous for being the toughest batter in history to strike out (114 whiffs in 7,132 at bats), also gave the company a tremendous compliment. After using the same Louisville Slugger for six or seven years before breaking it, Sewell sent the cracked bat to Hillerich & Bradsby along with a note that said, "Ha, ha! You didn't make any money off me!"

More than 180,000 people a year visit the Louisville Slugger Museum, and in his job as vice president of public relations Bill Williams has welcomed to the museum a wide variety of visiting celebrities (including rock star Alice Cooper and actor James Doohan—"Scottie" of *Star Trek* fame) as well as the prop men from numerous film projects seeking to obtain authentic Louisville Sluggers for use in their movies. The museum also receives a large volume of mail; much of it from youngsters who like writing to Louisville Slugger almost as much as they like writing to the North Pole. "When we get twenty-five letters from kids attending the same school, we know it's a class project," says Williams. "A lot of times the only address on the envelope is 'Louisville Slugger Bat Company,' but the letters always get here.

"One letter I'll never forget came from a little girl, who wrote: 'You make the best bats in the world. They are my favorite animal.'"

Inside the Louisville Slugger Museum are a number of interesting artifacts, displays, and exhibits, but perhaps its most eye-catching object is to be found outside, leaning up against the building—a 120-foot-long Louisville Slugger, the longest bat in the world. According to Williams, "The twin spires of Churchill Downs racetrack will always be the symbol of Louisville, but the bat has become a close second."

The bat, made of carbon steel and weighing 68,000 pounds, was engineered and fabricated by Caldwell Tanks, a local manufacturer of water tanks. Five layers of paint were used to cover and seal the entire bat, including a hand-painted wood-grain coat. The bat is an exact-scale replica of Babe Ruth's model R43 bat, which he used in the early 1920s, but the signature of Bud Hillerich appears on the barrel in tribute to the founder of the company. Just getting the bat to where it is today took a carefully orchestrated plan—city streets were closed and two flat bed trucks were hooked together—which required special permission from the state of Kentucky. It took six hours to transport the bat from where it was made, a distance of twelve miles, and raise it into place. Although the bat is self-supporting and does not actually lean against the museum, the designers wanted, for the sake of realism, to give the impression that it does, for that is what bats do in children's closets and players' lockers.

Because the company also wanted the bat to look like a real bat, it took great pains with the paint job. "We were concerned that it would look like the bat outside Yankee Stadium," says

Williams, "which is not painted to replicate an actual bat as ours is. One day after the bat had been painted, I took my mother, Anne, to have a look at it. The bat was lying on its side in a field surrounded by a fence. When my mom saw it, she said, 'Lord-a-mercy, honey, how did you ever find a piece of wood that big!' When she said that, we were no longer concerned."

CHARLIE MANUEL

With a lifetime batting average slightly under the (Mario) Mendoza Line of .200, Charlie Manuel didn't exactly have a sterling career as a major leaguer, yet he became the type of manager that most players love to play for.

According to pitcher Tom Kramer, who played for Manuel at Colorado Springs in 1991 before Manuel became the skipper of the Cleveland Indians, "Charlie was a good guy in the clubhouse and in the dugout. He loved coaching, he loved the players, and he loved to joke around. Most managers are always serious and on edge, especially when the team is losing, and they don't like to hear much laughter in the dugout. But Charlie liked to keep everybody loose and felt that we'd play better if we were loose.

"Charlie was always saying something funny, and he talked with a West Virginia drawl and a little bit of a stutter, which made everything he said sound even funnier. He was always giving people goofy names. He called Jeff Shaw "Shawball," he called me "Kramepiece," and he called Louie Medina "Funky Cold Medina" after the rap song of the same name. One game Louie struck out four times, and when he came back to the dugout after his fourth whiff, Charlie said, 'Dang, Funky Cold, if I didn't know better I'd swear you had a bet on us losing today.'

"Another time Jerry DiPoto was pitching for us, and Albuquerque was pounding the daylights out of him, beating us 10–2. Almost every day in Colorado Springs we'd get a little rain shower in the afternoon, after which the sun would come back out. Well, it hadn't rained yet that day, so Charlie stood on the top step of the dugout and, looking back at the mountains behind us, said, 'Damn! Where's that rainstorm. A flood's the only thing that's gonna save DiPoto today.' DiPoto and Charlie almost got into it when the inning was over because Jerry, who was a real competitor, got mad when he looked in the dugout and saw everybody laughing at what Charlie had said while he was out there getting his brains beat out.

"At some point that season the Indians called Jeff Shaw up to Cleveland, and some of the veteran pitchers on our team got upset about it. They were grumbling, saying things like 'I don't need this. I'm going home. That shows no respect to me to call up some punk kid instead of me.' One of these guys was so mad he snubbed Charlie—didn't say hello to Charlie when he passed by. Charlie got tired of listening to them complain, so he called a meeting of the pitchers. He said, 'I've got two things to say. One, if you want to get called back up to the big leagues, pitch better. Two, crying about Shaw getting called up is not going to help you any. And three, . . .' When he said that, it was all I could do not to start laughing, because he'd started out saying he had two things to say. The third point he decided to make was, 'If I say hi to you, you say hi back because you're no better than me.'

"Charlie wasn't that good with the pitchers, but he was great with the hitters. His teams always hit. He'd say, 'You pitchers—just hold the other team down a little bit because you know we're gonna hit their pitchers.' Charlie just loved hitting. He loved teaching it, he loved watching batting practice, and he loved home runs. For him that's what the game was all about. He liked to kid me by saying, 'If I could have faced you a couple of hundred times, I'd still be playing in the big leagues.' Charlie loved watching good hitting so much that he even pretended to want to see the other team's hitters crush the ball. One time he was going over the stats in the dugout, looking at how many home runs each of us had surrendered. He got to Jeff Shaw's line on the report and said, 'Shawball—eight home runs. You'll give up more long balls than that.' Then he looked at my total and said, 'Kramepiece, you've only given up two home runs. Next time we play Albuquerque, I want you to give Mike Piazza one right down the middle. I want to see how far he can hit it.'

"As he said that, he made a knocking 'home run' sound with his tongue off the roof of his mouth, he put one hand up to his right eye as if he were looking through a telescope, and with the other hand he made a motion as if he were pulling the telescope out to its full length so he could follow the flight of the long distance home run I was going to throw to Piazza. I just laughed and said, 'Okay, Charlie.'"

WILLIE MAYS

Willie Mays has always been a favorite in New York, where he played for the Giants and the Mets, but on at least one occasion his celebrity proved to be troublesome for one of his fans, as the following story told by Chuck Harmon illustrates.

"Willie and I were good friends," says Harmon, "and whenever the team I was playing for would go into New York to play the Giants, Willie and I would get together after one of the games and go out to dinner. One day I met Willie after a game,

and he had this beautiful girl with him who was going to go out to dinner with us. When I say that this girl was beautiful, I mean that she was a real show stopper—a Marilyn-Monroe-with-the-wind-blowing-her-skirt-up kind of girl.

"Anyway, the three of us were walking down the sidewalk when a couple came past us heading in the opposite direction. Just as we passed each other, the man turned around to look back at us. The next thing we knew the woman had hit the man upside the head with her pocket book and was hollering and cussing at him. See, she thought the man was trying to check out Willie's girl. The man said, 'Honey, that's Willie Mays! That's all I was looking at.'

"And she said, 'I know what you were looking at, and when you're with me, I'm the only woman you better be looking at.' The guy tried to defend himself, but it didn't do any good because the woman he was with didn't know who Willie was. So Willie got that poor guy in trouble just for being himself."

BILL MAZEROSKI

Second baseman Bill Mazeroski of the Pittsburgh Pirates became famous for one swing of the bat: his leadoff home run in the bottom of the ninth inning against Ralph Terry to win the seventh game of the 1960 World Series. Maz's surprising blow defeated the mighty New York Yankees, universally considered to be the superior team; drove the entire city of Pittsburgh into a frenzy of celebration; and forever burned into the consciousness of fans everywhere the image of Mazeroski fighting off crazed fans as he rounded third and headed toward ecstatic teammates waiting for him at home plate.

The stunning home run, the most dramatic ever hit in the World Series, was grand enough to serve as the highlight of any player's career. Ironically, it tended in later years to hamper Maz's chances of being elected to the Hall of Fame, as some voters, who felt that the historic home run resulted in an overestimation of Mazeroski's worthiness as a candidate for baseball's ultimate shrine, underestimated the true value of his extraordinary fielding. In the voting done by the nation's sportswriters over a fifteen-year period, Mazeroski never came close to being elected to the Hall of Fame. Although Maz won eight Gold Gloves, led the National League in major defensive categories thirty-five times, and set the record for double plays by a middle infielder (1,706), his accomplishments as a fielder were not enough for the sportswriters. The Veterans Committee saw things differently. They recognized his genius as a fielder and, nearly thirty years after he had retired, voted him into the Hall of Fame.

Mazeroski was set to be inducted into the Hall of Fame on August 5, 2001. It was not difficult to imagine how much the honor would mean to Mazeroski, but no one could have predicted how much his acceptance speech would mean to everyone else.

Inductees, who sometimes wind up rambling a bit, are asked to limit the length of their remarks to fifteen minutes. Bill Mazeroski didn't come close to that standard either. Overcome by feelings of gratitude and humility, he was in trouble from the very first moment. "I knew this was gonna happen," he began as he fought back tears. "I've got twelve pages here," he said, referring to his prepared remarks, "But it's hot, so I probably won't say half of this stuff."

Pausing often and battling the entire time to control his emotions, Maz managed to get out only snippets of his prepared speech:

"Baseball meant everything to me. If I'd never made the major leagues, I'd probably be playing for some bar for peanuts and cigarettes. It just so happened I was good enough to play in the big leagues. I wouldn't have changed anything. Hank Aaron was in Pittsburgh a couple of years ago, and he told me he thought I should get in. I didn't think a hitter like Hank Aaron would look at me as a Hall of Famer. So when he got on the Veterans Committee, I thought I had a chance. I think defense belongs in the Hall of Fame. Defense deserves as much credit as pitching and hitting, and I'm proud to be going in as a defensive player. I want to thank the Veterans Committee for getting me here. I thought when the Pirates retired my number, that would be the greatest thing to ever happen to me."

The allusion to his beloved Pirates, the only team he'd played for in his seventeen-year major league career, was more than he could handle. "I don't think I'm gonna make it," he choked. "I want to thank everybody who made the trip up here to listen to all this crap." And that was it. He couldn't continue. The

shortest, but most memorable, speech in Hall of Fame history was over. He managed to get out "Thank you to everybody!" as he left the podium, the tears flowing freely now, and sat down.

The crowd of twenty thousand fans spread over the grounds of the Clark Sports Center rose as one and gave Mazeroski a thunderous ovation. Many people in the crowd wept joyously right along with him, and then a rare thing happened: the other Hall of Famers on the podium stood and applauded too. And more than a few of them also needed to dab at the corners of their eyes.

Minnesota great Kirby Puckett was also inducted that day, and in his speech he tipped his cap to Mazeroski. "If you didn't shed a few tears at Maz's speech, you don't have an emotional bone in your body," he said. Later, in the post-induction press conference, Kirby revealed that he kiddingly told Maz, "Your wife is going to kill you" for leaving her and the kids out of his aborted speech.

It didn't solve any of major league baseball's recurring problems, but Maz's brief remarks showed that some players do love and respect the game the way we think all players should. For a few moments anyway, the speech, like a fresh breeze, cleared away some of the cynicism fans have grown accustomed to feeling. And it proved that, contrary to Tom Hanks's famous line in the movie *A League of Their Own*, there is indeed crying in baseball.

MARK McGWIRE

When Roger Maris knocked 61 balls out of the park in 1961, he set a single-season home-run record that stood for almost four decades. Most observers thought that his mark would be bested by a single home run or possibly two, if it were ever to fall at all. That's why Mark McGwire's assault on the Maris record so electrified the baseball world in 1998. His 70 home runs not only broke the existing record; they shattered it. The friendly competition between McGwire and the Cubs' Sammy Sosa, who also surpassed Maris's once-sacrosanct total with 66 dingers of his own, only added to the magnitude and memorableness of the great home-run-record chase of 1998.

McGwire's accomplishment didn't make him a hero just to baseball fans. Judging by the reaction of players such as Mike Cameron and Sean Casey to their encounters with Big Mac, he became a bona fide hero to his colleagues as well.

Chicago White Sox center fielder Mike Cameron robbed McGwire of a home run and actually apologized for doing so. In an interleague game between the Cardinals and the White Sox on June 9, 1998, Cameron raced over to the right center field wall at Comiskey Park, leaped up, and speared a McGwire drive that was headed into the stands. When Cameron reached first base later in the game, McGwire complimented him on the catch. "Great play, man," he said.

"I didn't want to do it," said Cameron, "and the fans didn't want me to do it either. You heard how they booed me."

McGwire replied, "Don't sweat it. You were only doing your job." He would have ended the year with 71 home runs had Cameron not "stolen" one from him.

McGwire was such a powerful hitter that players on both teams routinely stopped what they were doing to watch him take batting practice before games. Before a game between the Cardinals and the Reds, McGwire turned the tables on Sean Casey, complimenting the rookie on his swing after watching him take batting practice. Casey was so thrilled he could only manage to say, "Thank you, Mark. You aren't bad yourself." After regaining his composure, Casey found a photo of McGwire and asked the big slugger to autograph it. McGwire did more than sign the picture, inscribing it: "To Case: You have a great swing and a great career ahead of you. Your friend, Mark McGwire." While talking about the picture with Hal McCoy of *Reds Report* the following spring, Casey said proudly, "That baby is in the middle of my mantle at home."

The funny thing about McGwire's accomplishment is the liberating effect it had on people's imaginations. By going so far past the previous standard, McGwire let the genie out of the bottle, so to speak; and almost immediately pundits and commentators began to wonder how long the new record would last. Until he broke the Maris record, McGwire was always cautious in assessing his chances of doing so. When asked a year later if he thought anyone would ever be able to top him by hitting 71 or more home runs, he said, "That's a lot of home runs, but it is possible."

Even Todd McFarland, the man who paid more than $3 million for McGwire's seventieth home-run ball, had to agree that McGwire's record was not invulnerable. "If somebody gets too close to McGwire's record, I saw what Tonya Harding did a few years ago, so there are options," he joked, referring to the attack meant to disable Harding's figure skating rival Nancy Kerrigan.

Of course, McGwire's record did fall a mere three years later, when Barry Bonds hit 73 home runs.

While Bonds was finally recognized as one of the greatest players in the history of the game, his record-setting perfor-

mance did not entrance the nation the way McGwire's had. There were many reasons for this: One was that McGwire's record was squashed before it had a chance to grow into a legend. Also, the ultraprivate, self-concerned Bonds was nowhere near as fan-and-media friendly as McGwire had been. But perhaps the key factor was that statistics proved that the overall home-run frequency in the major leagues had increased dramatically, for a number of reasons, in the years between 1993 and 1998, and again in the years between 1998 and 2001. As unfair as it may have been to Bonds, many fans simply concluded that the home run had been seriously cheapened. If there was any doubt about this, it was removed when Bonds's 73rd home-run ball went on the auction block in the summer of 2003. It wound up selling for only about $500,000 and was bought by the same collector who had purchased McGwire's 70th home-run ball (for six times as much): Todd McFarland.

JACK McKEON

Currently the manager of the Florida Marlins, Jack McKeon has spent a lifetime in professional baseball as a player, manager, scout, and front-office executive. He was dubbed "Trader Jack" for the numerous, often blockbuster, deals he made as vice president of baseball operations for the San Diego Padres during the 1980s. It was McKeon's acquisitions of players such as Terry Kennedy, Garry Templeton, Steve Garvey, Rich Gossage, and Graig Nettles that made the Padres capable of winning the 1984 National League pennant, the franchise's first ever. As a field manager, the cigar-chomping McKeon tried to make the game fun for his players. And his players, especially the younger ones, have almost always responded positively to his leadership. There is an exception to every rule though, and in this case the exception was Bill Faul, a pitcher on the Triple-A Omaha Royals' squad that McKeon managed in 1969.

Faul, a stocky, fireballing right-hander, was a bit of a strange bird. He didn't like to shower, believing that bath water washed away the body's natural oils; he carried a pistol with him on road trips; and he indulged in self-hypnosis before pitching, a strategy he had picked up while toiling for the Chicago Cubs. Faul was not a comfortable person to be on the bad side of, and for some reason he absolutely loathed Jack McKeon.

McKeon had known that he wasn't exactly Faul's first choice of someone to take out to dinner, but he was shocked when he discovered the true intensity of Faul's feelings toward him. One day when the Royals were batting and McKeon was coaching third base, the opponent's third baseman slapped a tag on a

Royals base runner that McKeon thought was excessively rough. Trader Jack registered his opinion of the play, he and the third baseman got into it, and in seconds the third baseman's teammates were swarming all over McKeon. Faul rushed out of the Royals' dugout, knocked the other team's players out of the way, and dragged his manager to safety. Back in the dugout McKeon expressed his gratitude: "Thank you, Bill. You saved my life out there."

"I told you. I'm gonna be the one who kills you," growled Faul darkly.

THE MINOR LEAGUES

For ballpark promotions awash in unadulterated tackiness, it would be difficult to top the one run by the Jacksonville Suns in Florida in the summer of 2001. On June 29th the team brought disgraced figure skater Tonya Harding to Wolfson Park, where she signed two thousand miniature black bats given away by the team. The twenty-two-inch bats were a not-so-subtle allusion to the infamous black baton that a thuggish associate of Harding's then-husband used in his attack on the knee of Nancy Kerrigan, Harding's chief skating rival.

As tasteless as the promotion was, Harding was a big hit, so to speak, as the crowd of 6,704 for the contest between the Suns and the Chattanooga Lookouts was swelled by a walkup sale of 2,500 tickets an hour and a half before the start of the game. Moreover, according to the *Florida Times-Union*, it took only twenty-six minutes for the team to distribute the Harding model billy clubs to two thousand local celebrity-starved fans. Not everyone was dazzled by Harding, however, and it is only fair to mention that her tossing out of the ceremonial first pitch was greeted by a mixture of cheers and boos.

All in all, though, the night definitely belonged to Tonya. Before leaving the ballpark she signed autographs for another hour, and she even spent the first inning of the game in the Suns' dugout, where she undoubtedly quizzed the players on the finer points of the game, such as how to throw a beanball and how to take out a defenseless second baseman on the double play.

Ballplayers have a lot of time to kill in the minor leagues, and it's inevitable that sooner or later they find themselves in sticky situations. Donnie Scott, a former major league catcher, who now manages the Dayton (Ohio) Dragons of the Midwest League, tells a story about finding himself in such a predicament when he was a player in the bush leagues.

"This happened when I was playing Triple-A ball for the Nashville Sounds," says Scott. "We were in Oklahoma City for a series against the 89ers, and after the game one night Terry Lee, our first baseman, and I were shooting pool in this bar connected to the restaurant that was in the Holiday Inn where we were staying.

"We'd only had two or three beers, and the place was almost ready to close. It was about twenty minutes to one. The dad of one of our players had come into town to watch us play, and he came over to Terry and me at the pool table. 'I bought you guys a couple of beers,' he said.

"'Hey, thanks a lot, Mr. So-and-so,' we said. I can't remember his name.

"Anyway, when the barmaid came over to us, she brought four pitchers of beer! 'Here's your beers,' she said.

"'Holy crap!' we said. Even though we only had a few minutes to do so, we finished off those pitchers—drank every drop. By then it was time to go, the place was closing up, and we were feeling pretty good. To leave, we had to walk through the restaurant, and as we were walking out we passed this open door that led into the kitchen. I stopped and looked in and saw that there was nobody there. I looked at Terry and said, 'Are you thinking what I'm thinking?'

"'Hell, yes,' he said. 'I'm starving, and you know we aren't going to find anything open at this time of night.'

"So we walked into the kitchen and right over to this big cooler. I reached in, grabbed four big hamburger patties, threw them on the grill, and fired that baby up. While I was cooking I told Terry to get out some stuff for the hamburgers, so he started digging around in the cooler for lettuce, tomato, onion, buns, the whole works. Man, I was really going at it, flipping those burgers, just as if I'd been the grill man at Wendy's.

"When I had the hamburgers about half done, this restaurant employee walked in. He didn't say a word, turned around, and left. A few minutes later the burgers were done. Terry had the buns all laid out, and I was just about to take the burgers off the grill and put 'em on the buns. Next thing I knew, this loud authoritative voice said, 'And just what in the——do you guys think you're doing?'

"It was two big cops who had been called by the restaurant manager. I tried to start explaining to him: 'Officer, we're pro ballplayers—with Nashville. We played the 89ers tonight. We didn't mean no harm. It's just that we're starving. And we're not stealing. We're gonna pay for the burgers.' I reached in my wallet and pulled out a $20 bill to show him. 'And I'm gonna clean the grill, too, when I'm finished. My momma didn't raise no slob.'

"None of this seemed to impress the cop much. He said, 'Are you guys staying here in the hotel?'

" 'Yes, sir. We are,' I said.

" 'Well, you've got five seconds to get out of here and get to your room for the rest of the night or you're going to jail,' he said.

"I started to argue with him just a little: 'Can't we at least take the hamburgers with us? They're done!' But Terry grabbed me and pulled me toward the door before I could get us into any serious trouble. And, needless to say, we went to bed hungry."

Ask Rochester Red Wings hitting coach Mike Hart to name the craziest thing he's ever seen in professional baseball, and he'll tell you, "That's easy. The thirty-three-inning game between the Red Wings and the Pawtucket Red Sox, the longest game in professional baseball history, that I played in on April 18, 1981. I was supposed to have the day off, but I pinch-hit in the eleventh inning and wound up batting eight times, going 1 for 6 with a couple of walks. Two future Hall of Famers played the whole game. Cal Ripken Jr. went 2 for 13 for us, and Wade Boggs went 4 for 12 for them. One of our outfielders, Dallas Williams, went 0 for 13, which is the worst oh-fer in baseball history. He came into the game hitting around .300 and dropped down to about .280."

The game, which started a half-hour late because of a temporary power failure at Pawtucket's McCoy Stadium, was actually suspended after thirty-two innings with the score tied at two. It was resumed sixty-five days later in Pawtucket and ended, ironically, after one more inning, with the PawSox winning it 3–2. After Rochester went down in order in the top of the thirty-third, the PawSox loaded the bases in the bottom of the inning and won professional baseball's longest marathon on a bloop single by first baseman Dave Koza. In all, the game lasted eight hours and twenty-five minutes, produced 213 at-bats and 60 strikeouts, and used 14 pitchers and 156 baseballs.

"The funny thing about it," says Hart, "is that we should never have played so long that night in the first place. There was a curfew at one o'clock, but they couldn't get hold of the International League president, Harold Cooper, to ask him about it. When they finally got hold of him, he said, 'What are you guys doing? Stop the game right now.' When we finally stopped playing, at the end of the thirty-second inning, it was 4:06 in the morning, and the sun was starting to come up. One of our pitchers, Luis Aponte, landed in the doghouse over that game. His wife thought he'd been out all night drinking and wouldn't let him into their apartment, so he had to come back to the clubhouse to spend the rest of the night there.

"McCoy Stadium at that time was a small ballpark, and a home run usually decided a game. But it was really cold and windy, and nobody could get one to go out. Sam Bowen crushed one for them, and I remember saying, 'That's gone.' But the wind blew it back into the park. I got my hit in the top of the twenty-first inning, and we scored a run to go ahead 2–1. We were going, 'Alright! We're gonna win now.' But they came right back in the bottom of the inning and tied it up again. So we kept on going and going and going, and one thing that kept us going was that guys on both teams were making great plays in the field, one after another. Neither team could score. For awhile we were so tired that we were playing sort of punch-drunk. I batted against Bruce Hurst around three o'clock in the morning, and he was fast to begin with; but I was so tired I felt like I was moving in slow motion, and Bruce's fastball seemed like it was coming in at two hundred mph. After a while, pride kicked in, and both teams started playing even harder. Neither side wanted to lose it. Somebody told us that the previous record in professional baseball was twenty-nine innings, and when we reached thirty we joked, 'Hey, now that we've got the record, let's keep going as long as we can and put the sucker out of reach.' Of course, once Mr. Cooper halted the game, nobody was mad about it. We'd all had enough. Only seventeen fans stayed for the whole game, and the Pawtucket front office gave them season tickets as a reward.

"It didn't really hit us until the next day just how historic the game was. People from the Baseball Hall of Fame were there to collect equipment used in the game and to have us sign baseballs. A poster was later made about the game and each of us players got a copy of it. As luck would have it, there was an afternoon game scheduled the next day at two in the afternoon. We just got to the ballpark, loosened up, and played. Everybody was too tired to even think about taking batting practice or infield.

"One interesting thing that very few people are aware of is that our catcher Dave Huppert caught thirty-one of the thirty-two innings we played that night. Not only that but, because of injury, he also had to catch the nine-inning game we played the next afternoon. Eddie Putnam, our other catcher, was finally sent up to pinch-hit for Dave in the thirty-second inning, but while Eddie was batting he strained a muscle in his forearm and couldn't play the next day.

"As a minor league coach, when I hear guys complain about catching a doubleheader, which is two seven-inning games, I know exactly what to tell them. I say, 'Let me tell you about a guy I knew who caught forty innings in less than twenty-four hours!'"

Some of the most eccentric individuals in professional baseball are to be found in the minor leagues, and one such character is sixty-two-year-old Marvin Gray. Gray is a sort of idiot savant who has worked for the professional baseball teams of Evansville, Indiana, for years. Gary Jones, the director of baseball operations for the Evansville Otters, knows Marvin well and tells an amusing story about one of his rare goof-ups.

"The first thing you have to understand about Marvin," says Jones, "is that even though he is epileptic and possibly learning disabled, he is also a very capable person in many ways and an astonishingly capable person in others. For instance, Marvin knows more about high school sports in this state than anybody else alive. He has been keeping records and statistics of high school games in all the sports for decades, and it's not at all unusual for sportswriters to call him for information. He's famous in Indiana, and people all over the state know him and love him.

"Marvin is also quite a patriot, and he loves the American flag. In fact, he's an expert on flags. He knows everything there is to know about flags, and he has a big collection of them, both American flags and the flags of other countries. He's in charge of the flag here at Bosse Field, and we actually have him listed as 'Flag Chairman' in our media guide. I remember one holiday—I think it was a Memorial Day—when some lady came out to the game that evening and got on him for not flying the flag at half-mast. Marvin lowered the flag just to appease her, but he told me later that you're only supposed to fly it at half-mast until twelve noon, so he knew more about it than she did. He moved into Section 8 housing a few years ago and complained that there was no flag pole at the place where he could fly a flag. One of the well-to-do sports fans around town heard about his predicament and paid to have a pole installed outside his apartment. Not only that, there was also a big ceremony for the installation, and all kinds of federal, state, and local government representatives, including somebody from the governor's office, showed up for the ceremony.

"In addition to serving as Flag Chairman, Marvin has always done a number of jobs for us, such as stuffing scorecards with inserts, keeping the league standings board up-to-date, and locking up the ballpark at the end of the night. One night years ago, when the team was called the Triplets and played in the Triple-A American Association, I was at a local restaurant eating a late dinner after the game with my wife when I got paged. There was a message for me that said somebody had driven past Bosse Field and heard cries for help that seemed to be coming from the roof of the ballpark. I drove over, and, sure enough, when I got there I found two people trapped on top of the roof. They were the broadcasters with the Denver team, and they'd been locked in the press box. The team hadn't been able to find them after the game and had left town without them, so after I let them out these two radio guys had to scramble to get a different flight back to Denver. Boy, was I glad I didn't have to listen to their broadcast the following night!

"The next day I asked Marvin if he had checked to make sure everybody was out of the press box before locking up, and he swore that he had, even after I told him what had happened. Every so often after that, I'd ask him, just to kid around with him and to remind him not to let it happen again, 'Hey, Marvin, remember when you locked those two radio guys in the press box?'

"He would always say, 'No, I didn't do that,' until just a couple of years ago. He finally said that yes, he remembered doing it. I guess he decided that enough time had passed that I would no longer be mad about it. But, of course, I never was mad about it in the first place."

Every minor league baseball player has the same goal when he begins his professional baseball career. More than anything else in the world he wants to make the major leagues, to join that exclusive fraternity of the world's greatest players—even if it's only for a single pitch—so that he can say for the rest of his life that he'd been good enough to be a big leaguer. The goal is never easy to attain, and sometimes the pain is sharpest for those who come the closest without actually making it to the Big Show. Jacksonville Suns general manager Peter Bragan Jr. tells a story about just such a player.

"Terrell Hansen was a big, old right fielder we had who was a Dale Murphy–type player," says Bragan. "He could hit, hit with power, and run a little. He even resembled Murphy in the face a little bit.

"Terrell was a great kid, a wonderful guy, and everybody liked him and respected him. He was like a baseball version of John Wayne and strong as hell. He didn't talk much, but when he did say something—like, 'Come on, let's score some runs!'—the other players in the dugout listened because they physically feared him.

"He played for us when we were affiliated with the Montreal Expos. After he got traded to the New York Mets organization, he had a couple of good years with their Triple-A team in Tidewater. During one of Darryl Strawberry's suspensions, he got called up to sit on the Mets' bench for five days. In that situation a guy sits there for four days, and then you're supposed to play him on the fifth day—so that just in case he never gets called up again, he will have officially played in the big leagues. Well, Terrell sat there for four days, but the Mets' manager forgot to start him on the fifth day. He finally remembered about Terrell when the game was almost over. He was going to have him pinch-hit, but the last out was made with Terrell in the on-deck circle. He came back down and bounced around Triple A and Double A the rest of his career, and from then on you could see it affecting him. It was like a knife grinding in his chest. He'd be watching a major league game on television in the clubhouse, and he'd say, 'You see that guy there? He batted sixth behind me when I was batting cleanup.' Terrell always batted fourth on every minor league team he played for. Or they'd see some pitcher in the game who had just been promoted to the big leagues, and Terrell would say, 'Jeez, they called that guy up! He ain't got nothing but a rinky-dink curve. I hit two home runs off him in one game.'

"It was really a quirk that he didn't have a five- or six-year major league career, and he was really unlucky to have been traded to the Mets when Strawberry was in his prime. He stayed in baseball until he was thirty-two or thirty-three, and at the end he even played some Independent ball out in California. If he had batted just one time, he would have gotten some closure. He would have been able to say, 'I played in the big leagues,' and he would have retired earlier and gotten on with his life sooner. But he never got that one at-bat, and he never got that closure."

EDDIE MURRAY

At the end of his twenty-year major league career, first base-man Eddie Murray knew he was going to be elected to the Baseball Hall of Fame. With 3,255 hits and 504 home runs, he joined Hank Aaron and Willie Mays as the only players in history to belong to both the 3,000-hit and 500-home-run clubs.

Murray was also very much aware of his reputation as being standoffish and uncooperative with the media. At the beginning of his acceptance speech in Cooperstown in the summer of 2003, Murray said, "When Ted Williams was inducted thirty-seven years ago, he said he must have earned it because he knew he didn't get in because of his friendship with the writers. I guess I'm proud to be in his company in that way." Murray went on to explain that while he may not have been Mr. Charming with the press, he didn't have anything against the writers. He simply regarded them as one more distraction he needed to block out in order to focus on doing his job. "I had to do what I had to do to make myself successful," he concluded without apology.

There was something else that contributed greatly to Murray's success: his ability to hit from both sides of the plate.

In 1975 when Murray was playing for the Asheville Orioles of the Double-A Southern League, his manager Jimmy Schaffer started working with him to turn the young slugger into a switch-hitter. Other people in the Baltimore organization told Schaffer, "Don't do it, you'll get fired." Schaffer didn't listen to the warnings. "I believed in the value of what we were doing," he says, "and, more importantly, Eddie believed in it."

Murray distinctly remembers the day when there was no turning back from the experiment. "I was going up to bat, and Jimmy called me back to the dugout," says Murray. "I couldn't imagine what he wanted, but I knew he wasn't going to pinch-hit for me. He asked, 'Are you ready to hit left-handed in a game?'

"I said, 'Sure.'

"Jimmy said, 'Go ahead and do it then.'

"When he said that, I got the biggest smile on my face, and I went up there and hit the first pitch I saw for a double. And the rest, as they say, is history.

"How important was my learning to switch-hit? Well, I don't think I would have made the Hall of Fame without learning to do it. I would have been good—because I could do some things with the bat right-handed—but I don't think I would have put up the numbers that got me into the Hall of Fame."

In 1977 Murray became the American League Rookie of the Year, but he wasn't even expected to make the major league team going into spring training. Toward the end of spring training, some of the writers in the Orioles' camp started asking manager Earl Weaver which minor league team in the Baltimore system was going to get Murray for the start of the season. Weaver told them, "Every time he plays in a game he gets a couple of hits. His team might be right here." The next day Murray hit a gargantuan home run over the center-field fence at Miami Stadium, assuring his place on the Orioles major league roster.

Murray started the 1977 season as the Orioles' designated hitter because the O's already had a veteran first baseman, Lee May.

It wasn't long, though, before Murray's outstanding fielding—he eventually won three Gold Gloves—brought about a reversal of their roles; a change that was foreshadowed on the very first day of batting practice at spring training.

May and veteran outfielder Pat Kelly were standing around in the outfield shagging fly balls while Murray was taking his cuts in the batting cage. The two of them marveled at the way the ball jumped off the rookie's bat. Kelly said, "I hope he's not an outfielder."

May said, "I hope he's not a first baseman."

The two veterans trotted into the dugout as Murray finished hitting in order to see what kind of glove the youngster had. When Murray picked up a first baseman's mitt, Kelly smiled and gave May a look that said, "Uh-oh! You're in trouble now!"

JOHNNY OATES

In the major leagues there is a proper way to do just about everything, including signing baseballs. On balls that all members of the team will be signing, each player usually signs on the same spot over and over again. The best and easiest place to sign a baseball, the so-called "sweet spot," is the middle of the panel that does not have the printed signature of the league president on it. The sweet spot is always reserved for the manager of the team, a lesson Scott Klingenbeck learned the hard way when he was a rookie with the Baltimore Orioles in 1994.

"I made my major league debut at Camden Yards against Detroit," says Klingenbeck. "I started the game and was fortunate enough to beat the Tigers with a little help from the bullpen. After the game I was real excited to have the game ball from my first major league win, and I asked my catcher, Chris Hoiles, to sign it for me. He asked me where I wanted him to sign it, and without thinking about it I told him to sign on the sweet spot. I signed the ball too and then put it in my locker so I could talk to the media. While I was talking to the sportswriters, Mike Mussina took the ball around the locker room and got the whole team to sign it. After the writers left, I picked up the ball and realized that I needed the signature of our manager, Johnny Oates, so I took the ball into his office and asked him to sign it.

"Johnny looked at the ball and said, 'Why is Hoiles on the sweet spot?' That's when I realized that I'd goofed up.

" 'Well, he caught the game and he called the pitches I threw,' I said, trying to come up with an excuse.

" 'That's true,' said Johnny with a smile, 'but I'm the one who called you up from the minor leagues.'

"I didn't have any comeback to that, and Johnny knew that I knew I'd messed up. He went ahead and signed the ball, but he did it in a way that made sure I'd never make the same mistake again: he signed his name right on top of my name."

ED OTT

Former Pittsburgh Pirates catcher Ed Ott was not a player to be trifled with. The college wrestling champion was strong as an ox and really knew how to handle himself; as New York Mets second baseman Felix Millan found out the hard way. Late in a 1977 game Millan jammed the baseball into Ott's face in retaliation for Ott's hard slide into second. Ott immediately lifted Millan overhead and then body-slammed him into the ground, breaking Millan's shoulder and ending his major league career. "I didn't mean to hurt the guy," Ott said afterward, "I just had a flashback to my wrestling days."

Ott's toughness and readiness to mix it up were appreciated by all his teammates, but especially by the Pirates' pitchers. Stringbean reliever Kent Tekulve, in particular, knew he could count on Ott when things got hairy. "Otter was kind of like my personal protector," says Tekulve, "because he was not only my roommate, he was also my best friend. We named him 'Troll,' after one of those mythical creatures that hide under bridges, because he was short and stocky and ornery. He always told me he'd give me one thousand dollars if anybody on the other team ever got to the mound before he did when I was pitching.

"Nobody ever did, although a few guys, like Rowland Office of the Atlanta Braves, tried. This was in 1979, the year the umpires went on strike. One day in May we were playing in Atlanta and had the substitute umps. They were really bad, number one; and number two, they completely lost control of the game. They made one bad call after another, against both teams. There were four bench-clearing brawls, and they ejected five players and five managers and coaches before it was all over. It was a mess.

"I was sent in to pitch the ninth inning with us holding a big lead. The inning before, Gene Garber of the Braves had hit Dave Parker with a pitch because Dave had hit a home run earlier in the game. I was told to get the first two guys out and then hit the third batter. Garber was due to hit third, but we knew that they would pinch-hit for him. I got the first two outs, and then the Braves sent up Rowland Office to bat for Garber.

"Rowland hadn't been playing, so he was pouting to begin with. Then, they sent him up to bat in a meaningless situation when he suspected he was going to be the designated target. He wasn't a happy camper. I didn't have a problem with plunking Office, but because I was a right-handed submariner, it was difficult for me to come that far inside to a left-hander like him. Otter set up inside, but my first pitch went over his head and hit the backstop. I got another ball, tried again, and that pitch, too, went over Ott's head. Office definitely knew then what was going on, and he got pissed that I was throwing at him. Ott was pissed, too, that I wasn't able to hit Office.

"Anyway, as soon as Office started out to the mound, Otter grabbed him. Office wanted to throw his batting helmet at me, but Ott had his arms pinned, and all Rowland could do was kind of fumble it toward me. For once in that game, the umps acted quickly and decisively. They tossed me out of the game, and they tossed Office out, too. As I was leaving the field, I saw Ott with Office's helmet. Otter wanted to fight some more, and he was so frustrated that there wasn't going to be any more fighting, he was trying to break Rowland's helmet. He bent the ear flap in, but it wouldn't snap off, and he got this crazy look on his face over it. All I could think of was that Office should have been glad that he'd been thrown out so that Ott was destroying his helmet and not him. Nevertheless, after the game, I got on Ed in the clubhouse about the helmet: 'What kind of weakling, are you, anyway? Can't even break a guy's helmet!'"

RAFAEL PALMEIRO

Rafael Palmeiro is one of baseball's least-known superstars. Everybody knew that the Cuban-born All-American out of Mississippi State could hit for average, but nobody expected him to develop into the kind of power hitter who would eventually hit 500 home runs, a milestone Palmeiro reached on May 11, 2003, while playing for the Texas Rangers. The 500-home-run club only has nineteen members, and if Rafael keeps up his current batting pace into the 2005 season, he will join an even more exclusive fraternity and become, along with Hank Aaron, Willie Mays, and Eddie Murray, the only players in history to amass at least 500 homers and 3,000 hits. The quiet Palmeiro has not exactly been swamped with endorsement opportunities during his career, but he did receive a check for $500,000 from the makers of Viagra for becoming, as he put it while talking to Street & Smith's *SportsBusiness Journal*, "the first player to admit that his bat was corked."

Scott Klingenbeck, who broke into the major leagues with the Orioles while Palmeiro was also playing for Baltimore, tells a story about another big fat check that Rafael received.

"This story begins in 1995 when I was called up to Baltimore from the Orioles' Triple-A farm team in Rochester," says Klingenbeck. "Because the Orioles wanted me in Baltimore immediately, I didn't have time to drive my car down from New York, so I had it shipped down. Now, the car I was driving was a 1989 Pontiac 6000. I'd gotten it from my dad, who'd bought it from the company he worked for. The car had some miles on it, but it still ran great.

"I was in Baltimore about a week when Palmeiro came over to my locker in the clubhouse and said, 'Hey, kid, you can't be driving that junker into the players' parking lot at Camden Yards anymore. You're in the big leagues now.'

"I said, 'Rafey, I have to drive it. I don't own any other car.'

"He said, 'You can't drive that piece of crap. That's it. End of discussion.'

"'Well, what am I supposed to do then?' I said.

"'Here,' he said, tossing me some keys, 'drive my Hummer.' He'd done a commercial for the local Hummer dealership, and they'd given him a new Hummer to drive all summer as part of the deal. But he didn't need it, because he already owned several expensive cars. I didn't want to drive his Hummer because the thing was too big and cumbersome, and I was afraid I was going to run into another car with it; but I had no choice. Palmeiro had taken my car keys out of my locker, and he wouldn't tell me where they were.

"A couple of weeks later we were on a plane starting a road trip. The traveling secretary walked through the plane handing out paychecks and envelopes full of meal money. A bunch of guys sitting around me started talking about a bonus check for two million dollars that they knew Palmeiro was going to get. Kevin Brown, one of our starting pitchers, wanted me to tear up the check and offered me one hundred dollars to do it. 'Come on, Scott, do it,' he said, as he pulled a big wad of bills out of his pocket. 'I'll give you a hundred bucks if you do it.'

"I wanted to do it, but I was kind of afraid to, being a rookie and everything, so I thought I would ask Harold Baines what he thought, because he was such a level-headed, straight-up guy.

Harold said, 'Go ahead if you want to. They'll just issue him a new check. The only one who'll get upset about it is the club accountant.'

"So I decided to do it. All the guys asked to see the check and took turns looking at it. I sat down next to Palmeiro and asked to look at it too. I said, 'Hey, Rafey. I can't believe how much money this is. You're rich, man! How about giving me one thousand dollars of it.'

"Palmeiro said, 'Man, I can't do that. I've got a family to support, and I'm building a new seven-thousand-square-foot house in Texas.'

"'Oh, come on, Rafey,' I said. 'Gimme just a thousand bucks. That's nothing.' I turned to Kevin Brown and said, 'If you had a check for two million dollars, you'd give me a thousand, wouldn't you, Kevin?'

"Kevin said, 'I sure would. And I'll give you a hundred bucks right now if you do something we talked about.'

"I asked Rafey one more time, and when he ignored me I said, 'Okay. You give me no choice. Since you won't share, there's only one thing I can do.' And with that I tore that check for two million dollars up into little pieces. Everybody started laughing like crazy, except for Palmeiro, who stood up and started walking to the front of the plane, where all the coaches and the front-office brass were—to tell on me, just like a school kid.

"When he came back, he told me that Mr. Angelos, the owner of the team, wanted to see me. I went up to the front of the plane, and as I passed by the coaches they all gave me a "You're in trouble now!" look, but I was pretty sure they were just trying to scare me.

"All Mr. Angelos did was ask me why I tore the check up. I told him that I did it for two reasons: one, the hundred bucks that Kevin Brown had just given me; and two, that damn Hummer I was having to drive around in, like a tank, because

Palmeiro had stolen my car keys. Mr. Angelos wrote out another check right there and made me take it back and give it to Rafey. 'You better not tear this one up,' he said.

"It didn't quite make us even, but I did get a measure of revenge for having to drive that damn Hummer around. And I did get the keys to my Pontiac back later that summer when I got traded to Minnesota, but I didn't drive the car anymore. I guess Rafey had been right all along, because as soon as I got settled in Minnesota I went out and bought a vehicle more in keeping with my big league status: a Jeep Grand Cherokee."

LOU PINIELLA

Young fans may know him only as a manager, but the Tampa Bay Devil Rays' Lou Piniella was a darned good major league player in his day, and a smart one, too. The play that best exemplified Lou's high baseball IQ came in the one-game playoff between the New York Yankees and the Boston Red Sox at Fenway Park that decided the 1978 American League pennant. In the bottom of the ninth inning with the Yankees ahead 5–4 and Boston shortstop Rick Burleson on first, Red Sox second baseman Jerry Remy hit a liner toward Piniella in right field. Piniella lost the ball in the sun but coolly pretended that nothing was wrong. When the ball hit in front of him and started to bounce past him, Piniella took a desperate stab at it and caught it. The pantomime by Piniella prevented Burleson from moving up an extra base, which was important because the next batter hit a long fly ball that would have scored Burleson with the tying run had he been on third. One out later Burleson did get to third, but he died there when Carl Yastrzemski popped up, giving the Yankees the pennant.

When the situation demanded it Piniella could put on a poker face, but at the same time he was a fierce competitor, known for slamming down bats and slinging helmets. This intensity carried over to his managing career. The most infamous Piniella explosion came when he was managing the Cincinnati Reds in 1990. On August 21 Lou became so incensed during an argument with first base umpire Dutch Rennert that he uprooted first base and heaved it toward right field. Not satisfied with his first toss, he ran over, picked up the base, and flung it again—all to the delight of the crowd. Two days later the *Cincinnati Enquirer* made light of the incident by holding a celebrity base-throwing contest at lunchtime. Cincinnati Mayor Charlie Luken won the contest with a toss of 43¼ feet, and even television reporter Mary Krutko, wearing high heels, bested Piniella's effort, which supposedly had gone 35 feet.

This is not to suggest that Lou, while sometimes a hot head, does not also try to be fair. Jim Schaly, a substitute umpire in the American League for a brief time in 1995, tells a story that illustrates both sides of Piniella's personality. "Piniella was managing the Mariners at the time," says Schaly, "and I was on the bases at third for a game in Seattle, which was my first game in the big leagues. Now, I'm from Marietta, Ohio, home of Marietta College, where my dad has been the head baseball coach since before Abner Doubleday invented the game, and all my friends back home in Ohio were staying up late to watch the game.

"There was a close play at third that went against the Mariners. The Seattle third baseman missed the tag, and so I called the runner safe. Piniella came out and argued like hell for five minutes. He really got in my face and, although I didn't back down, it was embarrassing.

"After the next inning was over and they were showing commercials on television, Piniella came out and said, 'I just thought I ought to tell you that Joe Morgan, who's broadcasting the game upstairs, saw the play on replay, and he called down to the dugout to tell me that you got the play right and for me to leave you alone.'

"I said, 'That's great, Lou. Thanks a lot. But would you mind telling that to everybody in Marietta, Ohio?'"

POSTAGE STAMPS

Who are the two greatest baseball players in history? Babe Ruth and Jackie Robinson—at least judging by the stamps issued by the United States Postal Service. Ruth and Robinson have both appeared on U.S. stamps three different times, giving them a one-stamp lead over runners-up Roberto Clemente and Lou Gehrig.

Baseball first appeared on a U.S. stamp in 1939, when a group of boys playing a sandlot game was depicted on a three-cent stamp to commemorate the supposed one hundredth anniversary of the invention of baseball in Cooperstown, New York. The next U.S. baseball stamp was issued in 1969 to commemorate the one hundredth anniversary of professional baseball, and it wasn't until 1982 that the first specific baseball players, Robinson and Clemente, received the honor of being depicted on U.S. stamps. Even then, the USPS, evincing some hesitancy in recognizing ballplayers simply for their athletic accomplishments, couched the honor in cultural terms: the Robinson stamp was part of a Black Heritage series, the flag prominently displayed in the background of the Clemente stamp calls attention to Clemente's status as Puerto Rico's greatest hero, in any realm of endeavor. In one sense, then, Babe Ruth in 1983 was the first player to be recognized on a U.S. stamp simply as a great baseball player, and Lou Gehrig in 1989 was the second.

Ruth and Robinson became the first baseball players to enjoy a USPS encore when they became part of the Celebrate the Century series, a set of ten fifteen-stamp sheets issued between 1998 and 2000 that commemorate, decade by decade, "the most significant people, events, and accomplishments of the twentieth century." For hitting 60 home runs in 1927, Ruth was included as being representative of the 1920s, while Robinson was recognized on the 1940s sheet for breaking baseball's color barrier.

Ruth and Robinson, along with their philatelic pals, Clemente and Gehrig, were honored again in 2000 when the USPS issued a series of stamps depicting twenty different players. The twenty were all among the one hundred finalists for the All-Century Team, but only half of the twenty players appearing in the "Legends of Baseball" stamps actually had been selected to the final All-Century Team of thirty players. The USPS was only able to use ten of the All-Century Team and had to select ten "second stringers" (Hall of Famers all) for their stamps. It had to do this because the other twenty members of the final team were still living at the time, and postal regulations forbid any living person from being represented on a stamp. Still, the "Legends of Baseball" sheet is clear proof that the USPS is no longer squeamish about issuing stamps that honor baseball players as greats of the diamond and nothing more—which is good news for those of us who look forward to seeing more baseball heroes of the past helping move our mail from place to place.

KIRBY PUCKETT

The youngest of nine children, Kirby Puckett grew up in one of the worst gang-infested public housing projects in Chicago, yet he became one of the most positive people to ever play major league baseball. The Puckett family lived on the fourteenth floor of their dilapidated building, and because the elevators seldom worked the family would form a human chain in order to pass bags of groceries up the stairs to the Puckett apartment. Despite being born into such difficult surroundings, Puckett was determined that "I wasn't going to be a product of my environment." Kirby discovered baseball at the age of five, and the game became his passion. He played baseball and kids' makeshift versions of the game at every opportunity, even in the dead of winter when he would shovel snow off the sidewalks in order to play a little catch. He also received encouragement from his selfless parents. The Pucketts never had much money, but they always managed to get Kirby the one birthday present he asked for every year: a new baseball glove.

Puckett's habitual optimism served him well when he became a major leaguer and even had a great effect on the outcome of the 1991 World Series. The Atlanta Braves' lopsided 14–5 victory over Puckett's Minnesota Twins in Game Five gave the Braves a three-to-two advantage and demoralized Kirby's teammates. When Puckett walked into the Twins' clubhouse prior to the start of Game Six, the place "was like a morgue."

"Damn, guys," Puckett said. "Nobody died. We're still alive."

Kirby called his teammates together and told them, "Guys, I want you all to jump on my back because I'm going to carry

us tonight." Puckett's teammates erupted in a cheer and just like that, recovered their self-confidence. True to his word, Puckett went out and almost single-handedly beat the Braves: hitting an RBI-triple in the first inning, making a great catch in the third, driving in another run with a sacrifice fly, and hitting a game-ending solo home run in the bottom of the eleventh. Somebody else was the hero in Game Seven, but it was the inspiration provided by Puckett that won the World Series for the Twins.

Even after his career was ended prematurely by glaucoma, Kirby Puckett maintained his infectious optimism. On the day he was inducted into the Baseball Hall of Fame, he told fans, "It may be cloudy in my right eye, but the sun is shining brightly in my left eye."

DAN QUISENBERRY

As a pitcher at little La Verne College in California, Dan Quisenberry was not a stud. He didn't get drafted his senior year, but his college coach Ben Hines believed he deserved at least a chance in pro ball, and so he got on the phone and stayed on the phone until he found somebody willing to give Quiz a chance. A Kansas City Royals scout finally said yes and had the young man sign on the dotted line for what you'd pay a kid to cut your grass all summer, five hundred dollars.

It was the best investment the Royals ever made. Quisenberry kept throwing submarine sinkers, minor league hitters at one level after another kept beating them into routine grounders, and within five years Dan was with the Royals. Major league hitters couldn't hit him either, and he became for a period of six years the best short reliever in the American League. Quisenberry led the American League in saves five times, made the All-Star Team three times, pitched in two World Series, and finished with a total of 244 saves and an ERA of 2.76. The whole time he was in the major league spotlight Quisenberry displayed a mind that was as quirky as his pitching delivery, and he became famous for one funny line after another, such as his observation that "The greatest thing about baseball is that there is no homework." Often, he was the target of his own good-natured humor. "I lull them into a false sense of security by letting them watch me pitch," he said once. "If overconfidence can cause the Roman Empire to fall, I ought to be able to get a ground ball." Another time he compared himself to reliever Goose Gossage, who threw gas, by saying: "Gossage comes in and slams the door. I just close

the door quietly." When he hung up his spikes, sportswriters mourned as they hadn't since the retirement of Casey Stengel, the old Professor.

Financially secure and apparently with all the time in the world to do whatever he chose to do, Quisenberry decided to start writing poetry. The people who knew him best weren't surprised that he got into an endeavor involving one's innermost thoughts and feelings. Some of his poems were about baseball, but others were about topics more traditionally found in poetry: love, family, nature, the meaning of life, and death. Some of the baseball poems he sent to *Spitball: The Literary Baseball Magazine*, which I edited. We chose three of his poems for publication, and we had our cover artist, Donnie Pollard, execute a pen and ink drawing of Quiz at work on the mound for the issue in which the poems appeared.

A couple of years later I visited Quisenberry in Kansas City. I was in town for the National Convention of SABR (the Society for American Baseball Research). When he pulled his SUV up in front of my hotel, I told him, "We can talk here, in the lobby or in my room, but I think it only fair to warn you that there is a convention of four hundred baseball historians going on in the hotel." With a look of genuine alarm that had never crossed his face on the mound, even when he stared down the barrel of Reggie Jackson's Louisville Slugger, he said, "Get in. Let's go somewhere else."

He drove across town to a different hotel. As we walked through the front door of the place, he said hello to the bellhop, who smiled and addressed him by his first name. We took a table in the restaurant, and for the next two hours, while he relaxed in relative anonymity, he quietly told me baseball stories and reminisced about favorite people from his baseball past. Like Gary Blaylock, the Royals' pitching coach. Quiz recalled how Blaylock constantly had a coffee cup in his hand and the smell of coffee on his breath. One time Blaylock, who often led philosophical discussions on the art of pitching, proffered the opinion that a pitcher should always pitch to his strength. A Royals pitcher countered, "Yeah, but I'm a low-ball pitcher. What do I do when I face a low-ball hitter?"

"Pitch lower," said Blaylock.

Quiz also remembered the sad day when Dick Howser, who was dying of brain cancer, addressed the team he had managed only a few months before. Quiz remembered Howser saying, "There's more to life than baseball." Under normal circumstances the statement would have been merely a cliché, but under these particular circumstances, it had a profound effect on Dan. Quiz later wrote a poem about the encounter, about the strangeness of it, about the players' discomfort with the obvious mellowing of the team's former leader. He entitled it "Ode to Dick Howser." It was collected in Quiz's first and only book of poetry, *On Days Like This*, along with twenty-one other baseball poems and twenty-eight other poems on a variety of non-baseball topics.

And then one day came the news, like a completely unexpected slap in the face, that Dan Quisenberry, too, had a brain tumor. A bad one. Dan took chemotherapy and lost his hair, but not his sense of humor or his zest for life. Doctors operated and removed 80 percent of the tumor, but it grew back to the horror of everyone who knew the Quiz, who had watched him pitch, who had laughed at one of his jokes.

Before he died, Quiz took one last trip to Kauffman Stadium. With his wife, Janie, and their children, David and Alysia, at his side, Quiz was inducted into the Royals' Hall of Fame on May 30, 1998. "I'm so blessed," he said into the microphone, as the tears streamed down the faces of the thirty thousand fans in attendance. Applause—no, love in the form of applause—shook the stadium when he circled the ball field in a maroon Corvette convertible, saying good-bye. As usual, he found something to joke about afterward. "I don't know why I was waving. I'm not running for office," he said.

Quiz's book of poetry was released in June of 1998. The publisher, Helicon Nine Editions, printed ten thousand copies, half of which sold within the first fourteen months, an astonishing record of sales for poetry in this day and age. On March 6, 2001, Helicon Nine Editions gave away two thousand of the remaining copies of the book at Kauffman Stadium to celebrate National Poetry Month and to honor the memory of the poet. It was the best souvenir ever given away at a Royals game.

CAL RIPKEN JR.

Among the many virtues and abilities that served Cal Ripken Jr. well during his pursuit of Lou Gehrig's record of consecutive games played was his high threshold for pain. That's because no one could play 2,632 straight games in the major leagues, as Cal did, without sustaining more than a few injuries. While none of Ripken's injuries were automatic streak-busters, several of them would have sidelined players with less grit, and Cal's ability to play through them testified to his toughness.

In a real sense Ripken was lucky that the injuries he did receive were for the most part minor ones. On the other hand, he wasn't so lucky when he broke his nose at the 1996 All-Star Game in Philadelphia. What made the accident the freakiest injury of his career was the fact that it occurred before the game, during the taking of the team picture.

White Sox relief pitcher Roberto Hernandez was the culprit who bloodied the nose of the Iron Man of Baltimore. While taking his place among the players who were lined up for the photo, Hernandez stepped onto the platform, and it tilted. In trying to keep his balance, Hernandez flung his arm backward, giving Ripken's nose a vicious backhand in the process. The first broken nose of Ripken's life was a bloody one, but he wasn't about to let it become his Achilles nose and prevent him from playing in his 14th consecutive All-Star Game. Ripken, in fact, pretty much reset the nose himself, so that by the time the Phillies' team doctor arrived to help, he needed to make only a minor adjustment. Ripken, who had been voted into the American League starting lineup, then proceeded to go out and, with

gauze stuffed up his nose, play the first six innings of the game, which was won by the National League 6–0. When asked about playing with the broken nose, he said, "I didn't give it a second thought."

Hernandez, who felt terrible for Ripken, was kidded about the repercussions of the accident by Cal's Orioles teammates on the AL All-Star squad. "Robbie Alomar and Brady Anderson offered to get me a bodyguard the next time I go to Baltimore," said Roberto.

PHIL RIZZUTO

When veteran baseball broadcaster George Grande worked in the New York Yankees' broadcast booth for a couple of seasons in the early 1990s, he couldn't have been more delighted that his partners were Hall of Fame pitcher Tom Seaver and Hall of Fame shortstop Phil "Scooter" Rizzuto. "I played college baseball with Seaver at the University of Southern California, and Rizzuto was like an uncle to me," says Grande.

Grande not only enjoyed working with Rizzuto, who is famous for his unpredictability and zany tangents on the air, but he and Seaver found a way to have fun with one of Rizzuto's idiosyncrasies. "The Yankees made light of the fact that Scooter never went down on the field to talk to the players," says Grande. "He stayed upstairs in the booth and told me and Seaver that it was our job to interview the players on the field.

"Well, one day we told him that, because we were going to do the opening of the show on the field, he'd have to come down out of the booth. So, I started to do the intro to the show, with Seaver and Scooter standing next to me, when pitcher Dave LaPoint came up and interrupted me. 'George, how you been?' he asked.

"I said, 'Fine, Dave.'

"And then LaPoint goes, 'Excuse me, sir, who are you? You're Phil Rizzuto? You mean, I finally get to meet the great Phil Rizzuto!! Hey, fellas, guess who this is?' And then the whole team came over as if they wanted to meet Scooter. We'd set him up, of course.

"A couple of weeks later we were in Boston, and there was this young guy who worked for a cable TV company. He interviewed Tom, and then he interviewed me. When we got ready to go upstairs, the young guy asked us if there was any chance of Mr. Rizzuto coming down. 'He might,' we told him.

"When Seaver and I walked into the broadcasting booth, we both had envelopes in our hands. I said, 'Hey, Tom, what'd you get in your envelope?'

"He said, 'I got a five-hundred-dollar American Express gift certificate. What'd you get in your envelope?'

"I said, 'I got the same thing you got: an American Express gift certificate for five hundred dollars.'

"'Where'd you guys get those?' asked Scooter.

"'Some kid who interviewed us,' we said. 'There he is, down there.'

"The next day the kid is still hanging around. Scooter goes down on the field, and the kid interviews him. And when the kid is finished, Scooter sticks his hand out. All the kid does is shake Scooter's hand, so when he lets go, Scooter sticks his hand out again.

"Right then we whistled and shouted, 'Hey, Scooter!'

"Scooter turned around and looked up and saw our big grins and knew that he'd been had again. 'You huckleberries!!!' he shouted."

ALEX RODRIGUEZ

Alex Rodriguez is the rarest of sports superstars: the phenom who actually lives up to his advance billing. In fact, Rodriguez, a sensational prep player at Miami Westminster High School in Florida and the overall number-one pick of the 1993 amateur draft, may have surpassed expectations; as many experts consider the smooth-fielding, power-hitting shortstop who seemingly does everything without effort to be the best all-around player in the game today. The Texas Rangers certainly thought so, and they spent like drunken U.S. Congressmen to prove it; signing Alex to a ten-year, $252-million free-agent contract in December of 2000 that made him, by far, the highest-paid player in baseball history.

With spectacular seasons in 2001 and 2002, Rodriguez proved that the Rangers were no dummies, and his actions at the 2001 All-Star Game showed that he still has his head on straight, despite having the wealth of a half dozen kings. A-Rod was voted by the fans as the American League's starting shortstop, yet when the American League players jogged out of the dugout at Seattle's Safeco Field to start the game, Alex did not go out to his appointed position. Instead, as a gesture of his respect and affection for the man who had been his childhood role model, he staked a claim to third base and motioned for Cal Ripken Jr. to go to short. Once the premier shortstop in baseball, Ripken had not played short since his move to third base midway through the 1997 season, and he hesitated to make the switch because he wasn't sure that the All-Star Game was "the time or place to go back to short." Nevertheless

Rodriguez insisted, saying, "Everybody's expecting you to do it. Go on over there." And so Ripken played shortstop one last inning to the delighted approval of the sold-out crowd.

Ripken, who moved back to third base in the second inning, drove the crowd into a frenzy in the bottom of the third by homering off Los Angeles Dodgers pitcher Chan Ho Park. The homer made Ripken, at forty years, ten months, and ten days, the oldest player to ever homer in an All-Star Game, and it earned him his second All-Star Game MVP Award. After the game, the home run was on everyone's mind, but Ripken didn't forget to thank Rodriguez for his thoughtfulness. "It was a really neat tribute," he said. "I spent most of my career at shortstop. It was great being at shortstop again. I appreciated it."

A-Rod was so good coming right out of high school that his brief minor league career can best be described as a courtesy call. Jacksonville Suns general manager Peter Bragan Jr. remembers watching the young Rodriguez make a play that convinced him that the Suns wouldn't enjoy the services of the kid for long. "Alex didn't even play pro ball the summer he got drafted after high school. His agent, Scott Boras, held him out—said that they didn't want to sign with Seattle in the first place—and had Alex ready to go to the University of Miami in the fall when they finally signed with the Mariners for big money. The next spring Rodriguez skipped rookie ball and went right to the Midwest League. He had an MVP-type season for Appleton, the first half of the season and earned a promotion to our ball club. The Mariners told Appleton, 'We hate to take him from you, but he needs to go up.'

"In his first game with us the manager had him batting seventh. We beat Greenville 1–0 in Greenville, and Rodriguez hit a home run to win it.

"In his fifth or sixth game with us we were at home when he made a play in the field I'll never forget. There were two outs with a runner on second, and he went deep in the hole to field a ground ball. As the runner on second rounded third, Rodriguez faked a throw to first. The coach on third base, who was the manager of the other team, waved the runner on to home. Rodriguez straightened up, let the runner take a few more steps toward home, and then gunned him out by ten steps. And when he did it, he had a big child-like grin on his face, as if he were just some kid having fun playing ball on the sandlots. Right then and there, I knew he was going to be something really special.

"In Seattle, the Mariners' manager, Lou Piniella, was saying, 'I can't win without the horses. We've got a kid in Double A in Jacksonville who can help us right now, but the front office won't let me have him.' The Mariners' general manager, Woody Woodward, didn't want to bring Rodriguez up to Seattle so soon, but after Piniella said what he said, his hand was forced. We had Rodriguez for seventeen games, and then he went to the big leagues. And the rest, as they say, is history."

PETE ROSE

Regardless of what anybody thinks about the controversy that led to Pete Rose's banishment from baseball, no one could ever accuse Rose of not always doing his best to give the fans their money's worth.

Years ago, in the heyday of the Big Red Machine, the Reds would schedule a preseason exhibition game against the Indianapolis Indians in Indianapolis. The game was considered a reward for the loyalty of Cincinnati's Triple-A farm club and its fans, but most of the members of the Reds' starting lineup did not relish playing in the meaningless contest. Nevertheless, manager Sparky Anderson required his starters to play long enough to bat one time, after which they could retire for the day and head to the golf course.

In one of these games between the Reds and the Indianapolis Indians, Rose made an out when he batted. But instead of heading for the showers, he told Anderson he wanted to stay in the game. The second time he batted, Rose stroked a single to right field. As the right fielder leisurely fielded the ball, Rose never hesitated rounding first. He kept right on sprinting toward second, slid head-first into the bag, well ahead of the right fielder's throw, and stood on the bag, dusting himself off as the sell-out crowd of Hoosiers showered him with a standing ovation.

In the dugout after the inning was over, Rose said to Anderson: "That's what they came for. Now you can take me out."

ADOLF RUPP

In the old days when major league players were not as rich as kings, they had to work in the off-season. Brooklyn Dodgers pitcher Max Macon earned money in the wintertime by officiating college basketball games, a job that led to a memorable encounter with Adolf Rupp, the legendary head basketball coach of the University of Kentucky. The story is told by Bill Zinser, Macon's officiating partner, who also scouted for the Cleveland Indians.

"One time Max and I did a game when Alabama beat Kentucky, at Kentucky, which never happened back then," says Zinser. "Kentucky got upset—and so did Adolf!"

"Now, coaches are not allowed to come into the officials' dressing room, but here he comes, barreling in, mad as a hornet whose nest has been whacked by a broom. Adolf was going to give us hell, but 'You guys' is all he got out. Max, who was a pretty big and strong guy, jumped up and told me, 'Bill, hold that door open.' Then he grabbed Rupp by the collar and the belt in his pants and shoved him right out the door, as Adolf was hollering, 'You can't throw me out of my own house!'

"There was a newspaper photographer out in the hall who saw this, and he got a picture of Max shoving Adolf out of our dressing room. Adolf told him, 'If you put that picture in the paper, you'll never come in this gym again!' The newspaper guy had some guts because the next day that photo was on the front page of the *Lexington Herald*. I know that, because somebody cut it out and sent it to me.

"We didn't hold any grudge against Adolf, though, because we understood that even great coaches like him sometimes get caught up in the heat of the battle. And Adolf was a good guy. We saw him a week later at Auburn, and everything was fine. But I'll never forget that night with Coach Rupp when Max was the bouncer, and I was the doorman."

CHRIS SABO

Former Cincinnati Reds first baseman Todd Benzinger remembers Reds third baseman Chris Sabo as a down-to-earth, straight-shooting guy who was never afraid to speak his mind, even in front of the team's owner, Marge Schott.

"Although we were World Champions in 1990, we had a rough year the year before that," says Todd. "Our manager Pete Rose got suspended from baseball, and we finished the season in fifth place, seventeen games out of first. Even before Pete got suspended, things weren't going so well, and at one point in July we lost ten games in a row. The next day we were getting ready to go out for batting practice, when somebody came into the clubhouse and said, 'Don't go out on the field yet. Marge wants to have a team meeting upstairs.' So all of us, about twenty-five guys, went upstairs to a conference room in Riverfront Stadium, and when we got there we had to sit in chairs arranged in a big circle, like we were going to have a therapy session.

"Marge started talking, saying things like 'Look, guys, we're going through a helluva time here. We gotta figure out what to do about it.' She asked some questions and made a few suggestions that nobody really responded to, and then she said, 'Have you guys thought about prayer?'

"Although a few guys sort of snickered when she said that, the room really got silent. Then Chris Sabo said, 'Prayer? God doesn't give a rat's ass whether we win or lose! The pitcher is praying to get you out; you're praying to get a hit. Who's He going to listen to?!'

"Everybody was sort of stunned for a second that Sabo would speak up like that, but then we all burst out laughing. We had to. The meeting went on for a while longer, and I don't remember what else was said, but we didn't do any praying. Nevertheless, I think Chris's remarks broke the ice and helped us relax, because we went out and put an end to the losing streak."

BILL SCHLESINGER

If players whose time in the big leagues was brief are said to have enjoyed "a cup of coffee," then Bill Schlesinger, who today runs the Pleasant Ridge hardware store in Cincinnati, which he inherited from his mother and father, had what may be described as a "sip of coffee." Bill got to bat in the major leagues exactly one time, yet his story is as interesting as that of many ballplayers whose careers in the majors lasted much longer.

"The fact that I even got a chance to play professional base-ball is amazing," says Schlesinger, "as I got cut from both my high school (Woodward) and college (University of Cincinnati) teams. The person most responsible for me getting a chance was a New York Yankees scout named Pat Patterson, and Pat didn't even sign me.

"Here's how it happened. When I was a kid, my dad knew all kinds of people in baseball, and Reds players used to come into our hardware store all the time: guys like Ted Kluszewski, Johnny Temple, Roy McMillan, Ed Bailey, Jim Greengrass, and Johnny Vander Meer. My dad knew a lot of scouts, too, and was real good friends with Pat Patterson, who had played for the Yankees in 1921. One day Pat asked me what I wanted to do with my life, and I told him that I wanted to play profes-sional baseball. My dad just laughed and said I was going to keep helping him run the hardware store, but Pat said that he'd come out to one of my men's summer league games to watch me play. We played once a week on Sunday afternoons. He did come to one of my games, and I had a good day—I hit two home runs and stole a couple of bases. Pat said, 'You've got two important tools, power and speed. They're hard to come by. I'll see what I can do.'

"Now, Pat never told me any of this—I've just figured all of this out myself—but I'm sure he talked to the Yankees about me, and they said no, they weren't interested. A couple of weeks later, in walked Denny Galehouse, who had pitched for the Boston Red Sox, the Cleveland Indians, and the St. Louis Browns. Galehouse was scouting for the Red Sox, and Pat had told him about me. Denny asked me if I was interested in playing pro ball, and when I said I was, he asked, 'Is your dad here? Let's talk to him.'

"Denny told my dad, 'I'm able to offer Bill a thousand-dollar bonus. All he's got to do is sign this contract. Whattaya say?'

"My dad said, 'There's many, many other teams interested in my son. We'll have to think this over very carefully.'

"I almost had a heart attack when my dad said that.

"Galehouse—God bless him—played along. He knew there was nobody else interested in me. He was a real gentleman. He said, 'I understand, Mr. Schlesinger. What if I come back in two weeks. Is that enough time for you to make up your mind?'

"I couldn't believe what my dad did. After Galehouse left, I said, 'Do you realize what you've just done? You've ruined my life! He's gone forever. He's not coming back in two weeks. He's never coming back! I should have signed.' And even though a thousand dollars wasn't very much money for a bonus, even back then, it seemed like a fortune to me.

"My dad said, 'Don't worry. He'll come back, and he might offer you two or three thousand dollars next time.'

"Well, I was worried, and I got so nervous about it that I started playing bad. I went 0 for 4 the next Sunday and 0 for 4 the Sunday after that. I was praying that Galehouse didn't see either of those games. Two weeks later, though, he did come back. 'Well, have you made up your mind?' he asked.

"My dad said, 'It was the toughest decision we've ever had to make, but we're going to go with the Red Sox.'

"'Oh, that's wonderful,' said Galehouse, 'just wonderful.' He pulled out the contract for me to sign and started looking in his pockets for a pen for me to use to sign the contract, but he couldn't find one. I had one, though, because I was ready to sign. I couldn't wait to sign that contract. 'Here's a pen, Mr. Galehouse. I've got one right here,' I said.

"My dad said, 'Hold on there, son. Wait a minute. We didn't say anything about the money. Maybe it'll be more than a thousand dollars.'

"Galehouse said, 'No, it's still a thousand.' So I signed, and after I did, I kept asking Galehouse, 'Are you really going to send me a thousand dollars? You're not pulling my leg, are you? Please, don't kid about this.'

"A couple of weeks later the check from the Red Sox came, and I was so happy to get it because I used it to pay off the car I'd bought, a 1961 Corvette. A week or so later Pat Patterson came into the store and asked what was new. When I told him that Denny Galehouse had come by, he said, 'Denny Galehouse? I've heard of him. He scouts for the Red Sox, I think.' Pat played dumb, but I knew that his fingerprints were all over the deal."

The Red Sox signed Schlesinger as a first baseman, but he was so bad at fielding ground balls during spring training that they converted him into an outfielder. They wouldn't have even gone to the trouble had he not impressed them with his first round of batting practice, when he hit a couple of line drives and a couple of 430-foot shots. After making it through camp,

Schlesinger got assigned to Wellsville, New York, where he hit .341, drove in 117 runs, and led the league with 37 home runs. Suddenly, he was one of the prizes of the organization, and that winter his dad's instincts paid better dividends than when he was originally signed.

"At Wellsville I made five hundred dollars a month," says Schlesinger, "which was a lot of money to me. That winter the Red Sox sent me a major league contract because they were afraid of losing me to another team, who could have claimed me had they offered me a contract for a higher league than Boston was willing to offer me. The contract called for fifteen hundred dollars a month, and of course I wanted to sign it right away, but my dad said, 'No, we need to send the first three contracts they offer back to them.'

" 'What! That's crazy,' I said. 'They'll get mad at me and cut me or something.'

"My dad said, 'No they won't. They expect us to negotiate. Let's ask Pat Patterson about it.' And sure enough, Pat said to send the first one back. 'If you sign the first contract they send you, they think that you don't think you're very good,' he said. 'Don't worry. Everybody does it. They won't be mad. Just say that the contract is unsatisfactory.'

"So we returned the first contract, and a month later the Red Sox sent one for two thousand dollars. I was ready to sign that one, but Pat said to return it too. 'Say you think you're still worth more money,' he said. So we returned that one too, and a couple of weeks later they sent one for three thousand dollars, and Pat said to sign it, which I did. And my dad was really happy and felt justified. 'See, you made two thousand dollars a month just by playing a little hardball!' he said."

Schlesinger's one at-bat in the big leagues was not spectacular in any way, but it was a memorable one. "The Red Sox really didn't know what to do with me that spring, so they took me north with them when training camp ended. I wasn't ready to play in the big leagues, so I basically just sat on the bench and watched the games from there. I had a routine where I'd take batting practice, carry my equipment back to the clubhouse because I knew I wasn't going to use it in the game, and then go settle down in the far end of the dugout with a bunch of candy bars, gum, and soft drinks to watch the game. I'd sit next to Danny Fitzpatrick, the clubhouse manager who treated me like a son and really looked after me. And I did this from Opening Day until May 4, 1965, when I made my major league debut.

"We were in Los Angeles playing a night game against the Angels at Dodger Stadium. Marcelino Lopez was pitching against us and beating us 7–0, when late in the game our manager, Billy Herman, told me to pinch-hit. I couldn't believe it, and Herman had to repeat himself. 'Come on, get up there and pinch-hit!' he said.

"I started looking around for my bat and my helmet but couldn't find them because they were in the clubhouse. Fitzy had to run into the clubhouse and get them for me. I put a doughnut, one of those weighted rings, on the bat I was going to use and started warming up by swinging it and another bat. When I got near the plate, I tossed away the bat I wasn't going to use and tapped the handle of the other bat on the ground to loosen up the doughnut. The doughnut wouldn't come loose. I starting pounding the handle on the ground, but the doughnut just would not come off. I was getting embarrassed about it, and I could hear the guys in our dugout laughing. The ump said, 'Do you need help with that?'

"I told him no, I didn't need any help, but I still couldn't get the doughnut to slide down the barrel of the bat. The ump said,

'I think you do need some help.' Buck Rodgers, the Angels' catcher, grabbed the bat and knocked it on the plate a couple of times and finally got the doughnut loose. After I stepped into the batter's box, I remembered to check with the third base coach in case he wanted to give me any signs, so I stepped half way out of the box and looked down there. The ump said, — 'Look, kid. It's 7–0 and you're getting your ass handed to you. I've got a dinner date in one hour, and you're not going to make me late for it. Nobody's giving you any signs. Now get in the box and hit.'

"Rodgers said, 'Hey, kid, I hear you're a fastball hitter. You're in luck because this first pitch is going to be a fastball.' It wasn't. It was a curveball, and I looked silly swinging at it. So Rodgers lied to me. He said he was sorry and that the rest of the pitches would be fastballs, and they were. I did put the ball in play, but it wasn't much. I chopped a ball straight down off the plate, and Rodgers fielded it and easily threw me out at first. When I got back to the dugout, Fitzy said, 'Don't tell anybody you grounded out to the catcher.'

"After the game our manager, Billy Herman, said, 'I'm going to make you our Midnight Hitter.'

"'What's that mean?' I asked him.

"'It means that it was nine-thirty out here in California when you went up to hit tonight. Back in Boston it was after midnight, and nobody was up listening to the game. They were all asleep. We're going to do the same thing from now on—have you bat when it's midnight in Boston so you don't embarrass the organization.'

"After that everybody started calling me 'Midnight Hitter.'"

Schlesinger had another unforgettable day in his career, and the second one is painful to remember. A few years after his comical major league debut, Bill found himself in the Philadelphia Phillies' organization, playing for the Triple-A Eugene Emeralds, just a step below the majors. In fact, the Emeralds' manager, Frank Luchessi, told Schlesinger that he was going to be called up to the majors the first of September along with Mike Schmidt, Greg Luzinski, Larry Bowa, and Denny Doyle. It had taken Bill five years in the minors, but he'd finally learned to hit the curveball, and at the time he was doing so well he had a chance to win the Triple Crown of the PCL. "You guys'll just sit on the bench for the last month of the season up there," said Luchessi, "but next year I'm going to manage the Phillies, and I'll give all you guys every chance to stick with the team out of spring training." Bill never got to make the trip back to the big time, though, because on August 20, 1969, a Larry Sherry fastball struck him in the face just below the left eye. The injury not only ended Schlesinger's season, it also effectively ended his career, due to a large blind spot that ruined his once-perfect vision.

Nevertheless, the next spring Schlesinger didn't go down without a fight. "I pretty much knew that my career was over, but I had to be sure. I wanted one more chance to make sure," says Bill. "The Phillies had released me, and that spring nobody else really wanted to give me a chance. A few teams were willing to let me go to spring training but only if I paid my own way. The only team that offered to pay my way was the Pittsburgh Pirates, so I went down to Bradenton where the Pirates trained. I worked out for ten days or so, and then in the first exhibition game I got to bat early in the game. The second or third pitch that was thrown to me came in high and tight. It nicked the bill of my helmet just enough to knock it off my head. The owner of the team, Joe L. Brown, who was sitting behind home plate, came running onto the field and hollering for the umpires to stop the game. When he got out to the home plate area, he told me, 'Bill, that's it. It's all over. You didn't see that pitch, did you?'

"I had to admit that I hadn't. 'It's not worth it, son. Baseball's not worth risking your life over. Here's your plane ticket home.' And that's how my baseball career ended. Every day I still wonder what might have been, but I guess it just wasn't meant to be."

GEORGE SCOTT

George Scott came up to the Boston Red Sox in 1966 and immediately made an impact, hitting 27 home runs and becoming just the second rookie first baseman to start an All-Star Game. He acquired the nickname "Boomer" for his ability to hit long home runs. Scott, who wore love beads around his neck and a batting helmet in the field (long before John Olerud did), also immediately had trouble controlling his weight, a problem that caused him a lot of grief with manager Dick Williams the following year. Even though the Red Sox were battling for the pennant, Williams benched Scott on several occasions for being just a couple of pounds too heavy. Ironically, Boomer led the team in triples (7) and finished second in stolen bases (10) that year.

Although he avoided the sophomore jinx, the slick-fielding Scott, who won eight Gold Gloves, was unable to fend off an attack by the Green Monster his third season. Trying to hit home runs over Fenway Park's close, but towering, left-field wall, Scott messed up his swing so badly that he managed to hit only .171 with 3 home runs in 1968. He slowly recovered, reaching 24 homers in 1971, but Boston grew impatient and traded him to Milwaukee, where he had his best overall season in the majors (36, 109, .285) in 1975, the year the Red Sox lost a seven-game World Series to the Cincinnati Reds. Boston's trading young Cecil Cooper to the Brewers in order to reacquire Scott near the end of his career only compounded the Sox's original mistake, as a 33-homer last-hurrah-of-a-season in 1977 by Boomer did not offset the loss of a future star such as Cooper.

Despite the Red Sox's mishandling of Scott, he is remembered fondly by the Fenway faithful, and for more than his slugging and stellar work around the first base bag. On one unforgettable occasion the typically mumbling Scott, who was not known for either his elocution or his eloquence, was asked to address a sell-out crowd at Fenway. When Scott spoke into the microphone an electrical short prevented his voice from being heard. After Boomer tapped the mic, the short was cleared up, and his voice carried loud and clear all over the ballpark when he asked a club official standing nearby, "Is the mother—— on?"

On the other hand, Scott did have a poetic line at his disposal that he often used after one of his booming home runs. "I hit that one into the night," he'd say upon returning to the Boston dugout. "That was a night ball."

MIKE SHANNON

Former St. Louis Cardinals third baseman Mike Shannon was a hometown boy and an outstanding high school athlete. The only Missouri prepster to ever be named the state's best player in both football and basketball, Shannon accepted a scholarship from Coach Dan Devine to play quarterback at the University of Missouri when Missouri was a national powerhouse, but he left after his freshman year to sign with the Cardinals.

I got to see Mike play in 1964 in the minors, in Jacksonville, Florida, where I grew up, right before he went up to the Cardinals for good. Like any kid would, I thought that having the same name as a major leaguer portended something special in my life, perhaps a career of my own as a major league ballplayer. By the time my college baseball career wound down at North Carolina Wesleyan in Rocky Mount, the birthplace of Negro League great Buck Leonard, I knew that wasn't going to be the case. Still, having the same name as the man who made room on the Cards for Roger Maris by moving from right field to third base served a useful purpose and continues to do so to this day. When I meet a baseball fan for the first time who does not want to clarify whether or not I am the ex-Cardinal who was known to his teammates as "Moonman," I feel that I can safely assume that that person's knowledge of the game is less than comprehensive. It saves me a lot of poking around in other people's brains.

Awareness of Mike Shannon is a reliable barometer because Mike did have more than a cup of coffee in the big leagues. He was a regular in the St. Louis lineup from 1964 through 1969 and retired prematurely in 1970—not because he could no longer play, but because he contracted a rare kidney disease. Two years later he joined Jack Buck in the Cardinals' broadcast booth, and their partnership lasted more than three decades. Shannon was not particularly glib, but his enthusiasm, idiomatic language, and thorough knowledge of the game made him popular with Cardinals fans. Behind the mic in 1998 when Mark McGwire hit his famous home run, he was equal to the moment, fairly shouting his call: "and the 1-1 to Big Mac—Swing!—a— Get up, Baby, get up, get up! Home run! He's done it again! Seventy home runs! Take a ride on that for history!"

Nevertheless, my Mike Shannon test is hardly foolproof, as I've learned the hard way. Years ago at a World Series party I hosted, we split into two teams for a baseball trivia competition. When the opposing team asked, "Which Cardinals player hit a home run in all three World Series St. Louis played in the 1960s?" I blurted out the most ironically incorrect statement possible: "Well, I know it wasn't Mike Shannon."

RAZOR SHINES

Minor league coach and former Montreal Expos player Anthony Raymond "Razor" Shines has one of professional baseball's most colorful nicknames. Shines acquired the moniker while playing junior college ball when one of his teammates at St. Augustine College in Raleigh, North Carolina, said that he hit the ball so hard he sliced up the air. When Razor went into the pros, he never divulged the origin of the nickname and preferred to let the curious assume that there was something sinister about it.

A great nickname alone does not carry a person very far, though, and there was much more to Razor Shines than a catchy handle. In fact, according to Indianapolis Indians president Max Schumacher, who has worked for the Triple-A ball club for nearly fifty years, "Razor Shines is not only the most popular player we've ever had in Indianapolis, but he is also a legend in the modern minor leagues. Razor was an extremely colorful player. He walked with a certain swagger, he talked a lot, and he was always upbeat, always positive, never negative. He was the kind of player you love if he's on your team and you hate if he's on the other team.

"Razor was also a great late-inning hitter. If you watched him in the first six innings of a game, you'd think he was just another player. But with the tying or winning run on base in the late innings, he was a superstar. It was remarkable how often he would produce in those situations. He lived for those situations. In 1986, when we won the first of four straight American Association championships, we needed a rally in the bottom of the ninth to beat Denver in the seventh and final game of the Championship Series. The rally culminated with a single by Billy Moore off Rob Dibble to win it, but earlier in the inning they walked Razor intentionally, and he was so mad he wasn't going to get a chance to hit that he slammed his bat down on home plate and broke it.

"In 1985 Razor spent most of the season in the majors with Montreal. He hurt his knee sliding into a base and had the knee operated on in the off-season. It took longer for the knee to heal than anticipated, and Razor didn't want to let Montreal know about the operation. So he played hardball with his contract—acted like he didn't want to sign for the money they were offering him. On July 4th of 1986 he came into my office and said that he wanted to play. I tried to get Montreal to sign him, but they were worried he wasn't in shape. So I made a deal with them. I said I would make him our bullpen catcher and pay him until there was an opening on the roster, and then after we activated him they would be responsible for his salary. Razor mostly played first and third base, but he could also catch.

"Our manager that year, Joe Sparks, didn't know Razor, and he wasn't sure how to take him. He was thinking, 'What's Max gotten me into with this guy?' A week or so after Razor joined the team; we did need another catcher, and so we activated him when the team was on the road—in Des Moines, I think. In the first two games Razor played in, he got hits in critical situations that led to wins, but it was his catching that really impressed Sparks. Because his knee still wasn't right, Razor couldn't get all the way down into a crouch. He was a stand-up catcher. Sparks said, 'That was the most courageous performance I've ever seen in pro baseball—a guy catching in a semicrouch like that.'

"As great as it was to have Razor playing for us, it was also just fun to have him around. He was what I call our "give-up pitcher," if you know what I mean. The give-up pitcher is the guy you bring in when you're getting beat 12–2 and you know you're not going to win the game. He's not really a pitcher but a position player who's willing to go out there and be a sacrificial victim in order to save the wear and tear on the arms of your starting pitchers. Even if he gives up five more runs in one inning it doesn't matter, and you appreciate the guy for being willing to take one for the team.

"Well, Razor actually did a great job as our give-up pitcher. Three years in a row he pitched an inning in that kind of situation, and each time he pitched it was three up and three down. I thought I would tease him a little bit, so I said, 'Razor, you've done a great job pitching for us, but I've noticed that you only throw fastballs.'

" 'I've got a great slider,' he deadpanned. Then he added with a big grin, 'But I haven't needed it yet!' "

SAMMY SOSA

If, as a popular television commercial says, "It's not nice to fool Mother Nature," it's also not nice when Mother Nature fools us. Just ask Chicago Cubs slugger Sammy Sosa, who was victimized by the unpredictable lady on April 2, 2003, in his attempt to hit the 500th home run of his distinguished career.

Sosa, who had been foiled in the season's opener the day before, was walked in his first two at-bats by New York Mets starting pitcher Al Leiter. In the sixth inning Sosa came to bat with two on, no outs, and the Cubs trailing 4–1. With the fans in the outfield bleachers standing and a representative of the Baseball Hall of Fame on hand ready to acquire Sosa's bat for posterity, Sammy took a big cut and drove one of Leiter's pitches toward the left-field bleachers and history. As he'd done on his previous 499 homers, Sosa spread his wings, took his trademark little hop into the air, and clapped his hands as the crowd roared. However, before he could really get into his home-run trot, a gust of wind blew the ball back into the stadium where it was caught on the warning track by left fielder Cliff Floyd.

Afterward, Sosa made no bones about having been cheated. "I put a great swing on that ball," he said, "I probably hit it too high. The wind stopped it." Leiter concurred: "I thought he hit it, especially when he did his little dance." Lost in everyone's deflated expectations was the irony that Sosa had been denied his 500th homer at Shea Stadium and not at the Cubs' home park, Wrigley Field, where the wind is notorious for interfering with balls hit into the air.

Although Sosa got two hits the next day, the Mets stymied him again, and the scene shifted to Cincinnati, for a three-game series between the Cubs and the Reds. Before the game on Friday, April 4, Reds starting pitcher Danny Graves stated that he was not going to pitch around Sosa, who had been walked six times in three games by the Mets. "Not to sound like a jerk or anything, but I'm not changing the way I pitch to anybody," said Graves.

As for Sosa, he fully expected to hit the big home run in Cincinnati, because he knew as well as anyone else that he has averaged a home run every 11 at-bats. In the end, though, Graves did not surrender number 500. He hit Sosa with a pitch in the first inning, struck him out the next time, and got him to fly out in his third at-bat. Reds reliever Scott Sullivan was not so lucky. He got ahead of Sammy 1-2 in the seventh inning, but left his fourth pitch to Sosa over the plate. Sammy drove it into the bleachers in right-center field for number 500, and this time there was no wind to negate his celebratory dance. With that home run Sosa became only the eighteenth player to ever reach this milestone. Afterward, Sammy admitted that finally hitting number 500 lifted a heavy weight off his shoulders. "Everyone has been waiting for this moment," he said. "Now, I don't have to think about it. I don't have to swing for a home run every at-bat." And, he might have added, he also doesn't have to worry about which way the wind is blowing.

SPORTSWRITERS

Before he took over an amateur men's over-thirty baseball organization called Roy Hobbs Baseball, Tom Giffen was a sportswriter. Tom served one of his stints in the business at the *Chicago Sun* and remembers a funny exchange between editor Lewis Grizzard and the venerable Warren Brown, a member of the writers' wing of the Baseball Hall of Fame, who began writing sports for Chicago papers in the early 1920s.

"Mr. Brown never came into the office," says Giffen. "He always sent his stories in by e-mail or fax. The problem is that they were riddled with clichés. After Grizzard would take all the clichés out, Mr. Brown's column would be reduced six to twelve inches. Well, Grizzard finally called Mr. Brown into his office for a talk because he felt that Mr. Brown wasn't getting the hint.

"So Grizzard says to Mr. Brown, 'Do you know what we've been doing to your stories?'

"'Yeah. You've been taking all the color out of them,' says Mr. Brown.

"'That's not color. Those are clichés,' says Grizzard. 'Sportswriters have been using them for decades. They're not new or fresh anymore. They've been around since the 1930s.'

"'Yeah, I know,' says Mr. Brown. 'I'm the guy who invented them. And since I did, I think I should be allowed to use 'em.'"

Every year at the Baseball Hall of Fame Induction Ceremonies in Cooperstown, New York, the J. G. Taylor Spink Award is given to a sportswriter in recognition of his contributions to the field. While winning the award is a great honor, the recipients are not, in the eyes of baseball fans, the heroes that players inducted into the Hall of Fame are. No one knows this better than the winner of the 2000 Spink Award, Ross Newhan, who has covered major league baseball in Southern California for four decades. During his acceptance speech Newhan told a story that demonstrates how transitory fame usually is for the best of newspaper sportswriters.

"Every winter longtime Cincinnati sportswriter Bill Phelan vacationed in Havana, Cuba," said Newhan. "When he died, Phelan asked that his ashes be sent to his best friend on the island, Pepe Conte. When Pepe received the urn full of Phelan's ashes, he asked himself, 'What am I gonna do with this?'

"After thinking it over for a while, Pepe decided to take the urn to what had been Bill's favorite bar in order to share a final drink with his friend. One drink led to another drink, and then one bar led to another bar. The next morning, Pepe realized that he'd left the urn on the bar at his last stop, so he hurried back to retrieve it. When Pepe asked the bartender about his friend's ashes, he was told that they had been swept out, with last night's trash and yesterday's newspapers. That is often the fate of baseball writers, and I assure you that winning this award is much, much better."

WILLIE STARGELL

Few players in baseball history have ever been as instrumental in leading a team to a championship as Willie Stargell, who was the heart and soul of the 1979 World Champion Pittsburgh Pirates. Stargell's season-long clutch play on the diamond earned him a unique trifecta of honors, as he became the only player to ever win MVP awards for the regular season, the playoffs, and the World Series in the same year. As important as Stargell's timely hitting was, his leadership extended far beyond the confines of the batter's box, as the following story, told by Pirates relief ace Kent Tekulve, illustrates.

"I came into the seventh game of the World Series in Baltimore in the eighth inning," says Tekulve, "and we were up 2–1. The Orioles had scored first in the third inning on a home run by Rich Dauer off Jim Bibby, but Willie had hit a two-run homer in the sixth to give us the lead. I came in with one out and runners on first and second. I got Terry Crowley to ground out to second, but the runners moved up, so we walked Ken Singleton intentionally to load the bases. That brought Eddie Murray to the plate. I knew that the World Series was on the line right then and there. If Murray got a hit and they scored a couple of runs, we were going to lose the game because we had the bottom of our batting order coming up in the top of the ninth. The whole World Series was riding on this one at-bat, which I realized was the most important at-bat of my life.

"All of this was going through my mind, as I stood on the rubber feeling pretty exhausted because I was pitching in my hundred-and-first game of the season. I was trying to psyche

myself up for the situation when I saw Willie Stargell come waddling over to the mound. I say he was 'waddling' because Willie weighed well over 212 pounds, although that's the weight he was always listed at. I didn't know what Willie wanted to say, but I figured he was going to give me some advice. And that was okay with me, because he was the only guy on the team who had played in the seventh game of a World Series before.

"So Willie says, 'Teke, the bases are loaded.'

"The Orioles were wearing those ugly orange shirts, so when I looked around I saw a human pumpkin on each base. 'Yep,' I said.

" 'Murray is the batter,' said Willie.

"Murray was 6'4", 230 pounds, and the bat looked like a toothpick in his hands. 'Yep, I see him,' I said.

" 'He's their number-four batter and a real dangerous RBI guy,' he said.

" 'Yep.'

" 'He's also a switch-hitter, so he's going to bat left-handed against you.'

" 'Yep.'

" 'Teke, I read an article in the paper today that said you have trouble getting left-handed hitters out.'

"At this point I looked at him as if to say, 'Geez, Willie, how much more bad news are you going to deliver in one visit?'

"Then he said, 'I'll tell you what we're going to do. I'm left-handed; I'll pitch to Murray. You go play first base.'

"When he said that, I lost it. I was laughing so hard at the mental image of Willie trying to pitch to Murray with the seventh game of the World Series on the line, that I turned around to face center field and put my glove over my face. When I got my laughter under control, I dropped a couple of expletives on Stargell and told him to get his ass back to first base. A couple of pitches later Murray hit a fly ball to right field. It was a miserable day and the field was sloppy—there wasn't a lot of grass in the outfield because the NFL Colts had been playing in the stadium. Dave Parker slipped a couple of times and almost fell down, but he caught the ball, and we were out of the inning. We scored two in the top of the ninth, and then it was over after I got the Orioles one-two-three in the bottom of the inning.

"Ever since then I've always been amazed at what Willie did. He went through that whole schtick just to get me to laugh and to forget about the seriousness of the situation for a moment. Can you imagine the reaction of the reporters in the clubhouse after the game had I given up a hit to Murray? They would have been all over Willie, asking him why he broke my concentration. The easy thing for Willie to have done was nothing. He could have just stood there like everybody else, thinking, 'Teke's over there on the mound. He's one of the best relievers in the National League. Let him do his thing.' But he didn't do that. He risked taking the blame, and it made me realize that he did what he did because he thought it was the right thing to do. And he taught me a lesson I've tried to live by ever since: Make decisions based on what is the right thing to do, not on what the personal consequences might be if things don't go as planned.

"The next year during spring training I ran into Keith Jackson, who had broadcast the World Series with Howard Cosell and Don Drysdale, and he asked me what Willie had said to me. They had seen me laughing like everybody else, but they had never found out what I was laughing about.

"Later that day the whole thing was fresh in my mind again as I was participating in that pitchers-covering-first-base drill that you do a million times every spring—as if you forget where first base is over the winter. There were about thirty-five pitchers and ten first basemen taking turns running this drill. At one point my turn coincided with Willie's, and when we were walking together to get back in line, I asked Willie if he remembered coming over to the mound to crack me up at the exact climax of the World Series.

"He nodded and said, sure, he remembered. Then I told him, 'I'll tell you what, Will: If you ever do that again, and it's not the seventh game of the World Series, I'm handing you the ball and you can explain it to Chuck! [Chuck Tanner, manager of the Pirates at the time]'"

KENT TEKULVE

Former Pittsburgh Pirates reliever extraordinaire Kent Tekulve never received much consideration for the Baseball Hall of Fame, but he's not losing any sleep over the matter. That's because while he was growing up as a tall, very skinny lad with bad eyesight, he never expected to play major league baseball. "I didn't exactly have the prototypical major league player physique," says Tekulve, "and I got my chance to play pro ball, not because I was drafted out of college, but because I was signed out of a tryout camp, of all things, which hardly ever happens today."

Nobody may have paid much attention to the gangly sidearm pitcher when he came out of Marietta College in Ohio, but Tekulve baffled hitters in the low minor leagues. It was also in the minors that he became a submariner. "From the very beginning, I'd always thrown the ball sidearmed," he says, "and until I got into pro ball nobody ever tried to change me—not even my dad, to his credit. When I first started in pro ball, my pitches outside the strike zone, just off the plate, moved a lot, while my pitches over the plate had a tendency not to move as much. In the low minors I was able to get the hitters to swing at those pitches out of the strike zone. When I moved up in the Pirates organization, the hitters started laying off those pitches and waiting for the pitches over the plate, and I started getting hit. An old scout figured out what was happening, and he had me change my arm angle in an effort to get the pitches I threw over the plate to move as much as the pitches off the plate. First, I went to three-quarters, but that was a disaster. Then I remem-

185

bered having seen Ted Abernathy, another submariner, pitch when I was a boy, so I went the other way and dropped down to a submarine style of pitching. I developed my own style of pitching based on that childhood memory, and it worked. I experimented with other things like my grip and pressure points on the ball, but going submarine is what enabled me to get to the major leagues.

"The only guy who ever tried to discourage me from pitching sidearmed was Harding Peterson, who was the farm director when I started with the Pirates in 1969 at Geneva in the New York–Penn League. As you may know, the year before, in 1968, the pitchers—guys like Bob Gibson and Denny McLain —had totally dominated major league baseball. In reaction to that, major league baseball did all sorts of things to negate the pitchers, stuff like lowering the mound, shrinking the strike zone, bringing in the fences, and putting in artificial turf. Well, Harding came around and said that guys throwing sidearmed should learn to throw three-quarter or overhand because sidearmers wouldn't be able to pitch in the big leagues anymore under the new conditions. I decided to keep doing what I was doing until it didn't work anymore. When we won the World Series in 1979, Harding Peterson was the general manager of the Pirates. After the Series we went to all sorts of banquets and dinners. Every time I had to get up and speak, I'd tell this story to kid Harding, and I'd conclude by saying something like: 'How can this guy be GM of the World Champions? The only guys from that team in Geneva to get to the major leagues were the two sidearm pitchers he said would never make it: Bruce Kison and me!' "

Although Tekulve set a Pirates record for saves (31) in 1978 and tied it the following year, he is best remembered by Bucs fans for the time he played left field. "We were playing in San Francisco at Candlestick Park," says Kent, "and it was the first game of a doubleheader. We had recently gone through tons of pitching, which I guess had something to do with what happened. I was pitching in the bottom of the ninth with a one-run lead, and there were two outs with nobody on. Jack Clark was the batter, and he was a dangerous hitter because he could tie things up with one swing of the bat. Well, Clark laid down the most perfect drag bunt you've ever seen. Bill Madlock, our third baseman, couldn't get it because he was playing left field, and I couldn't get it; so Clark reached first. That brought up Darrell Evans, a left-handed batter, who was going to be followed by Mike Ivie, a right-hander.

"Clark's gutless drag bunt pissed me off because I was afraid that our manager Chuck Tanner was going to bring in Grant Jackson to face Evans so we would have a lefty-versus-lefty matchup, which would cost me a save. Sure enough, I saw Chuck start out of the dugout, which pissed me off even more because Chuck was the type of manager who would never change his mind about taking out a pitcher once he left the dugout. Nevertheless, I was going to try to talk Chuck out of taking me out. I had my case all laid out in my mind, when he said, 'You're playing left field.'

"I was so stunned that for the first time in my life nothing came out of my mouth when I tried to talk. My jaw just dropped. I finally was able to say, 'What?'

"'Go play left field,' he repeated.

"I jogged out to left field, and as I did three or four other things were happening. Our left fielder John Milner was bent out of shape over the move, and as he walked off the field he was muttering, 'I can't believe I'm being taken out for Tekulve!'

Lee Lacy, another outfielder, was warming up in the bullpen, in case he had to go to left when I went back in to pitch. And on the mound Chuck Tanner and Grant Jackson were discussing strategy. Chuck said, 'How are you going to pitch Evans?'

"Grant said, 'I'm going to work him inside.'

"Chuck said, 'No. Evans is a pull hitter. Work him away'

"Grant said, 'I can't pitch him outside. Teke's in left field.'

"Chuck said, 'I don't care. Evans is a pull hitter and a dangerous one, so I want you to pitch him away.'

" 'Okay,' said Grant.

While this conversation was going on, Omar Moreno came over from center field to give me a crash course in playing the outfield, which was great because he was the best center fielder in the game. He was tossing grass up in the air and everything. I was getting the whole lesson, and I was standing there going, 'Yeah. Yeah.' The only problem was that everything Omar said was in Spanish.

"So I was out in left field, playing straightaway, and on about the third pitch Evans hit a routine fly ball right to me. A real can of corn. There wasn't another living soul within 150 feet of me, but I started waving everybody else off, as if somebody else was going to try to catch the ball, and then I made the catch. I've always accused Evans of hitting the ball to me on purpose because he was the ultimate pull hitter. He never hit to left field. He claims he didn't hit to me on purpose, but I don't believe him.

"Nowadays, after the last out of a ballgame, all the players on the winning team form two lines on the field and walk past each other offering congratulations. Back then, everybody would congratulate just the pitcher as he walked right to the dugout. At the end of that game, Grant Jackson thought 'What the hell is going on?' because nobody walked over to congratulate him. They all ran out to left field to shake hands with me!

"I'd never thought about it before, but I always wound up with the last baseball used in a game when I closed out a game. That was the only time in my career I had no idea what to do with the last baseball. I guess I should have given it to Grant, but I didn't, and to this day I don't know what I did with it.

"Now, remember, that game was the first of a doubleheader. Normally, no media was allowed in the clubhouse between games, but they made an exception in that case because all the writers wanted to interview me about playing left field. They asked me if I was nervous when I caught the ball. I said, 'What do pitchers do 90 percent of the time during BP?' We shag fly balls, millions of them during a season, and we get so bored doing it that we catch them behind our backs and between our legs just to make it interesting. So, no, I wasn't nervous. They also asked me if the switch had been planned, and I told them no, that Chuck had never mentioned it before. I didn't know if he'd thought of it on the spot, or if it was something he'd remembered another manager, maybe Whitey Herzog, doing. When the writers left, I went over to Chuck's office and said, 'Nice move, Chuck. It worked. But please say you'll never try that again.'

"Of course, because he got the last out, Grant got the save. Making the catch cost me a save, which I could have used to break my own Pirates record because I ended the year with thirty-one saves, like I had the year before. I actually considered dropping the ball to get the chance to go back to the mound and earn the save. Chuck said that if I had dropped it on purpose I wouldn't have lived long enough to get another save.

"We won the pennant that year by one game, so later on I'd tell the guys that I single-handedly won the entire thing, that my catching that fly ball was the most important play of the whole season."

Tekulve is also known as one of the worst hitters in major league history to ever drag a bat up to the plate. "Bad hitter? I think ten for fifteen is pretty good," he says. "That's ten hits in fifteen years. They were all singles, and you could have thrown a blanket over all of them, as every one of them was a little flare over the second baseman's head into short right field. Two of them were off Tug McGraw, the only guy I got in my book twice, which is something I never let him forget. I'm especially proud of the second one, which was off a screwball. We were both at the end of our careers when he gave up the second one, so the old rule that you throw nothing but fastballs to another pitcher went out the window.

"I could bunt, but I wasn't much of a hitter. I didn't even hit during batting practice. I'd bunt five pitches, and then I'd put my bat in the bat rack and go relax in the clubhouse. One time Chuck asked me why I wasn't taking batting practice, so I told him, 'Let's look at this logically. If the game is on the line, am I going to bat or are you going to send up a pinch hitter?' He said he would send up a pinch hitter. 'Okay, then. Let's look at what can happen if I take batting practice. One of three things can happen, and all three are bad. One: I swing and miss and hurt myself. Two: I foul it off and hurt myself. Three: I get hit with the pitch and hurt myself. There's no clause in my contract that gives me a bonus for even one RBI, so there's no need for me to kill myself in batting practice. Chuck really couldn't argue with that logic, so I never took batting practice again.

"How bad was I with the bat? Well, there was a standing five-dollar bet between Willie Stargell and Bill Madlock about whether or not I would be able to foul one off during each of my six or so at-bats each year. One said 'Yes,' and one said 'No,' although now I can't remember who said what. Whatever it was, neither of them ever bet that I was going to get a hit.

"Believe it or not, I batted one time against Nolan Ryan. I was in the game to save it, and Nolan was still in the game, too, even though we had scored some runs on him late. All that did was make him mad. When I went up to the plate, I stood as far back in the box and as far away from the plate as I could possibly get. Alan Ashby, the Astros' catcher, started laughing just to see where I was standing.

"Harry Wendelstedt was the umpire, and I told him, 'If it doesn't hit the ground, it's a strike—or I'll hit you with this bat.' This made Ashby laugh some more. The first pitch came in about a hundred mph and ten inches outside. Harry went, 'Strike one!' I said, 'Good job, Harry!'

"That at-bat was a case of a man knowing his limitations, and I was definitely not capable of hitting Nolan Ryan."

His anemic hitting never bothered Tekulve, because he knew where his value to the team lay. He was nicknamed "Rubber Band Man" because of his ability to pitch on a daily basis if necessary, and the song of the same name was played every time he came out of the bullpen at Three Rivers Stadium in Pittsburgh. Tekulve led the National League in appearances four times, and three times he made more than 90 appearances. He retired with 1,050 appearances (all in relief, a record), which left him at the time only 20 appearances short of tying Hoyt Wilhelm's all-time record. "Both Danny Murtaugh and Chuck Tanner would put me into the game at the drop of a hat," says Tekulve. "One time people started worrying about how much Chuck was using me. 'You're gonna wear him out—you're gonna ruin his arm,' they were saying.

"Chuck said, 'Hey, we're paying him for a hundred-sixty-two games, and he's only working ninety or so.'

"My comeback to that was, 'Yeah, maybe so, but you warm me up for the other seventy-two, so I do work a hundred-sixty-two games a year.'"

Although Tekulve came out of the bullpen more often than any other Pirates pitcher of his era, he didn't hang out there. "I mentally could not stay on top of the game for every pitch 162 times a year," he says, "so I would stay in the clubhouse, listening to the game on the radio, for the first five or six innings. After that I would go down to the bullpen and start paying attention to the lineups, the situation, the pinch hitters available to the other team, etc."

Since Tekulve was all business in the bullpen, he was seldom in the middle of the hijinks typical of major league bullpens. Nevertheless, he remembers being around for one such incident involving fellow reliever Dave Giusti. "This happened in a game that got out of control early. We were winning 9–0 in the fifth inning, so the guys started screwing around. Giving a player a "hot foot" is an old baseball prank, whereby you stick a few matches in some gum to the bottom of the player's shoe and then light the matches. Well, Giusti gave somebody a hot foot, and then the guy started chasing Dave around the bullpen. We had a bathroom right off the bullpen, so Giusti ran in there and locked the door. The guy who was chasing Giusti beat on the door and cussed him out. 'Come out of there, you gutless SOB,' he yelled, but of course Giusti wouldn't come out.

"The rest of us were bored with the game, so we got involved in the hunt for Giusti. The door to the bathroom was metal, and we noticed that it had a louvered panel at the bottom for ventilation. 'Aha!' we thought. 'We'll smoke his ass out.' So we stuffed some paper cups into this grate and set them on fire. They smoked a little bit but not enough to drive our prey out into the open.

"Well, wouldn't you know it—the other team started coming back on us, and before we knew it the score was 9–5. The dugout called on the phone, and they said to have Giusti warm up. We told him, 'Dave, it's 9–5 now, and you need to warm up.' He didn't believe us at first, but we kept telling him, 'We're not bullshitting you, Dave. We're in a ballgame now, and you need to get loose. We'll worry about the other stuff later.'

"He finally believed us and unlocked the door, but he couldn't open it because the heat from our little fire had swelled the metal door shut tight. The dugout called again: 'We told you to get Giusti up!'

"'Uh . . . we can't.'

"'What? Why not?'

"'Uh . . . he's busy.'

"Eventually, somebody else had to go in to pitch. Back in the clubhouse after the game, which we won, thank goodness, they wanted to ask Giusti why he wasn't able to warm up, and they realized that he wasn't in the clubhouse. That's when we had to tell them that he was still stuck in the bullpen bathroom. It took the grounds crew half an hour to get him out, which they finally did by taking the door off the hinges. Ordinarily, you'd get fined for not being available to go into the game when they needed you, but it really wasn't Dave's fault. We were the ones who got the team's closer stuck in the bathroom in the middle of a game when we tried to smoke him out by burning those paper cups."

BRETT TOMKO

While employed by the Cincinnati Reds, right-handed starting pitcher Brett Tomko showed that he had a sense of humor, as well as experience visiting the kind of junky souvenir shops that sell cheap merchandise to tourists.

After a game on July 1, 1999, when he pitched well but saw credit for the Reds' 2–1 victory over the Arizona Diamondbacks go to a relief pitcher out of the Cincinnati bullpen, Tomko hung a sign on his locker after the game that said: "I pitched seven innings and gave up no earned runs, and all I got was this lousy T-shirt!"

BOB UECKER

Catcher Bob Uecker spent six highly undistinguished seasons in the big leagues (1962–67) with the Braves, Cardinals, and Phillies. Uecker's record of 14 home runs, 74 RBIs, and a batting average of exactly .200—for his career, not one season—is entirely forgettable, yet he is one of the most popular figures in baseball history. Why? Because he has made millions of fans laugh for decades at his deadpan, self-deprecating humor.

"Mr. Baseball," as Uecker facetiously named himself, got his break in show business one night in 1969 when he opened for Don Rickles at Al Hirt's nightclub in Atlanta. Hirt was so impressed with Uecker's act that he convinced Johnny Carson to put him on *The Tonight Show*. Carson, like everyone else, thought Uecker was hysterically funny, and Uecker's second career took off, not like a dribbler off his own bat, but like a Mark McGwire home run. "Ueck," who wound up making more than one hundred appearances on the Carson show, also starred in a television sitcom called "Mr. Belvedere," appeared in numerous commercials ("I must be in the front row!"), enjoyed an illustrious baseball broadcasting career that began in 1971, and played the role of a radio announcer in the movies *Major League* and *Major League II*. (You may remember him saying, "juuuust a bit outside.")

In honor of his more than three decades of baseball broadcasting, Uecker was presented with the 2003 Ford C. Frick Award at the Hall of Fame Induction Ceremonies on July 27, 2003. Uecker was preceded in the program by the winner of the J. G. Taylor Spink Award for sportswriting, Hal McCoy of the *Dayton Daily News*. McCoy's acceptance speech was unusually moving, as he thanked numerous people who wouldn't let him quit the job he loved to do when a rare eye disease rendered him essentially blind. The crowd at the Induction Ceremonies knew what they were in for when Uecker stepped to the microphone and opened his remarks by saying: "In contrast to Hal, I was asked to quit many times."

Although he did briefly offer the typical thank-yous at the end, Uecker's entire speech was actually a comedy routine that had the usually-reserved Hall of Famers sitting on the stage behind the speaker's podium crying tears of laughter. Here are the funniest one-liners and jokes from the most hilarious speech that will ever be heard in Cooperstown:

- "The first ball I ever played with was actually a football, which my dad bought me. We thought it was defective, though. We couldn't kick it or pass it or do anything fun with it. Finally, a kindly neighbor came over and put some air in it for us.
- "The first sport I played at school was basketball. We were so poor I couldn't afford to buy an athletic supporter, so my mother made me one—out of a flour sack. The only problem with that was the players on the other team always knew exactly where I was going on the court because of the little trail of flour I left behind. It was also a little embarrassing because the front of my homemade jock said, 'Pillsbury's Best.'
- "I was a pretty good baseball player in high school, and the Milwaukee Braves signed me for three thousand dollars. That was a modest amount of money, but it was all my dad had, and the Braves took it.
- "The first game I played in the big leagues I played in Milwaukee, my hometown where I was born and raised. My mom and dad, my whole family, and all my friends were

there at the game, and everybody was waving at me and laughing. Our manager, Birdie Tebbets, came up to me and asked me how I felt. He said, 'You're starting today. I didn't tell you beforehand, because I didn't want to make you nervous.' I told Birdie I was fine, that I wasn't nervous at all. Then he said, 'That's great, Bob. By the way, the rest of us wear our supporters inside our pants.'

- "In 1964 the Braves traded me to St. Louis, where I won the World Championship for the Cardinals. When we got into the World Series, the team trainer injected me with hepatitis, so I could go on the disabled list and they could bring up a backup infielder to take my place on the bench.

- "Some catchers have trouble with the knuckleball, but not me. I learned early on how to deal with it. I just waited for it to stop rolling and then I picked it up.

- "One day in Atlanta I caught Phil Niekro, a knuckleball pitcher, when he pitched against his brother Joe, another knuckleballer, who pitched for the Houston Astros. Their folks were sitting right behind home plate, and I saw Mr. and Mrs. Niekro more that day than Phil and Joe did all weekend.

- "I would take my kids to the ballgame, and they would want to go home with a different player.

- "My boys were just like me. One time they were playing in their Little League championship game. One of them struck out three times, and the other one made an error that let in the winning run. I couldn't have been prouder.

- "Gene Mauch was one of the great managers I played for. He'd say, 'Uecker, grab a bat and stop this rally.'

- "I had great shoe and glove contracts. The companies paid me a lot of money not to be seen using their stuff.

- "Fans always liked to ask how long a dozen bats would last me, and I'd tell 'em, 'Eight to ten cookouts.'

- "I still think I should have gone into the Hall of Fame as a player.
- "As a player at the end of your career, you always know when it's time to move on. With me, I walked into the Braves' clubhouse before a game, and our manager, Luman Harris, came up to me and said, 'No visitors allowed.'
- "I thought they appreciated my work as a broadcaster until I looked down and saw that there was no cord attached to my microphone. Later, after I'd gotten a microphone with a cord, I learned that they were using my portion of the broadcast to jam Radio Free Europe."

UMPIRES

There is an unwritten rule in professional baseball that the catcher is never supposed to turn around to argue with the umpire. Most umpires will listen to a little griping, or "chirping" as it is sometimes called, from the catcher, but not if the catcher turns his head backward because then, the thinking goes, every fan in the ballpark will know what the catcher thinks of the umpire's ball and strike calls. Looking backward toward the umpire is considered to be tantamount to "showing up" or embarrassing the umpire and is usually grounds for ejection from the game.

There is at least one other reason not to look back at the umpire, as the following story told by former Pittsburgh Pirates minor league catcher Chad Epperson illustrates. "I was playing for Nashville in the Pacific Coast League," says Chad, "and one night the umpire was screwing the hell out of us. We were complaining, of course, and I guess he got tired of it. So when our pitcher threw a 3-0 pitch right down the middle, he called it a ball just to prove who was in charge. I started cussing him up one side and down the other, but I didn't turn around.

"When the next batter got ready to hit, I held my glove out with a real stiff arm as if to say, 'You have to hit my glove without me budging an inch or it won't be called a strike.' Well, that made the umpire mad, and he started cussing me out. 'You sorry so-and-so, don't you show me up!' he said.

"I turned around to cuss him right back, and boom!—a ninety-two mph fastball hit me in the back, right where I'd had my glove. Oh, man did that hurt! My legs felt like Jell-O, and I could hardly stand up.

"I also didn't get any sympathy from the ump. He said, 'Serves you right—and you're out of the game!'"

A nyone who hangs around with professional umpires learns to have respect for what they do and learns not to be too quick to question their knowledge of the game. Umpire Jim Schaly tells a story that illustrates what the men in blue are up against.

"Back in 1987 when I was umpiring a South Atlantic League game in Myrtle Beach, South Carolina," says Schaly, "we had a play where two runners wound up on second base at the same time, which obviously is not allowed. The rule is that when two runners occupy the same base, the lead runner is the guy who is entitled to the base, not the guy coming into the base.

"Both runners have a foot on the base, so when the short-stop tags the lead runner I yell, 'Safe!'

"The lead runner steps off the bag, and then the shortstop tags the second guy, who now is entitled to the base. Again, I yell, 'Safe!'

"The first guy steps back on the base, the shortstop tags him, so I say, 'Safe,' not even signaling this time. He steps off again, the shortstop tags the second guy again, so I say, 'Safe' again.

"Now the shortstop is really confused and getting frustrated, so he finally tags them both, real quick, while they both have a foot on the bag, and so I call the second guy out.

"It just goes to show you how the ballplayers don't know the rules any better than a lot of the fans."

It's inevitable that the umpires and the players will disagree on at least a couple of calls each game. Sometimes the number of disputed calls is more than a few, as the following story told by former Cleveland Indians pitcher Tommy Kramer about umpire Ken Kaiser illustrates.

"Kaiser was okay," says Kramer, "but he definitely missed pitches when he was behind the plate. And in one game in particular he missed a whole lot of pitches. We were playing the Rangers in Texas, and Nolan Ryan was pitching against us. Ryan didn't need any help, but Kaiser was giving it to him anyway, calling strikes on pitches we thought were clearly balls. Around the seventh inning Ryan threw a real low pitch, and Kaiser called it a strike. Our manager, Mike Hargrove, was really frustrated, and we were losing the game, so he finally lost his patience and started complaining about the pitch.

"Kaiser took his mask off and said, 'I miss one call all game, and you're gonna jump on me!'

"Grover was so dumbfounded at the statement that he couldn't talk. But you could see what he was thinking by the expression on his face: 'Miss ONE call! Are you kidding me?'"

Tommy Kramer will also never forget the first time he pitched with Kaiser behind the plate.

"It was the longest five-and-two-thirds innings I ever threw in my life," says Kramer. "We were playing in Milwaukee during my rookie year, and every borderline pitch I threw was a ball. I mean, every one of them. But I didn't say anything or make any faces or stare in toward home plate after those calls. Two of our veteran pitchers, Charles Nagy and Ted Power, had warned me about Kaiser. 'You can't complain against this guy, or he'll remember and hold it against you,' they said. 'You have to suck it up and just keep pitching.'

"So that's what I did. After the game our catcher, Junior Ortiz, came over to me and said, 'Don't worry about the game today. Kais told me to tell you that you passed the test. He said he'll be better for you next time.'

"That was great to know, and I appreciated Kaiser letting me know, but the thing is that I never had him behind the plate again."

GREG VAUGHN

Baseball has honored many pioneers through the years, but let us not forget Greg Vaughn, the man who broke the facial-hair barrier in Cincinnati.

The Reds' ban on facial hair—beards, mustaches, goatees, and long sideburns—dated back to the late 1960s when general manager Bob Howsam decreed that the Reds look razor sharp at all times in order to project the wholesome, all-American image that Howsam thought would be appealing to the team's culturally conservative Midwestern fans. Over the years the Reds lost out on talented free agent players who refused to come to town clean shaven, such as ace reliever Rollie Fingers, who simply would not part with his trademark handlebar mustache. However, it took the arrival of Vaughn, obtained in a trade with the San Diego Padres right before the start of spring training in 1999, to whisk the ban away.

As soon as the trade was made, Vaughn threatened behind the scenes to file a grievance over the ban with the Players Association, a maneuver industry insiders predicted would succeed. Publicly, Vaughn took a more sentimental approach that was calculated to soften up the "pro-family" owner of the Reds, Marge Schott. "I can't shave my goatee," he said. "My kids have never seen me without it." If these ploys weren't enough to cause Schott to lift the ban, the support of the fans, who sided overwhelmingly with Vaughn in a newspaper poll, was the coup de grâce for what general manager Jim Bowden afterward called "a very archaic rule." It also didn't hurt that the weak-hitting Reds desperately needed Vaughn's big bat in their lineup.

Before leaving as a free agent after the season, the goateed Vaughn produced as expected in 1999, slugging 45 homers and driving in 118 runs (both highs for the team); but his lasting contribution to Reds baseball remained in the locker room. Every time a Reds player looks in the mirror to comb his beard or trim his Fu Manchu, he has the goatee of Greg Vaughn to thank for the privilege.

MIKE VEECK

"The apple doesn't fall far from the tree, and neither does the nut." That's what some people would say about Mike Veeck, the son of Bill Veeck, the owner who became infamous for sending a midget (Eddie Gaedel) up to bat in an official major league game. Bill Veeck was a marketing and promotional genius who was way ahead of his time. He was castigated by the owners of other major league teams for subscribing to the revolutionary idea that fans should have fun at baseball games, even when the home team loses. To that end, Veeck introduced all sorts of gimmicks and stunts to baseball, such as the exploding scoreboard, off-the-wall giveaways, softball-style shorts for White Sox players, and Grandstand Manager Day, whereby St. Louis Browns fans determined the team's strategy by voting with "YES" and "NO" placards. The Lords of Baseball did their best to resist Veeck's influence, but his philosophy eventually prevailed, and his contributions to the game were belatedly recognized when he was inducted into the Baseball Hall of Fame in 1991.

Following in his father's footsteps, Mike Veeck got off to a rocky start but recovered nicely to become one of the most innovative owners and promoters in minor league baseball. In Chicago, young Mike's idea to stage a Disco Demolition Night at Comiskey Park proved to be too popular. White Sox fans got so excited at seeing a local DJ blow up a huge pile of despised disco vinyl between games of a doubleheader that they stormed out of the stands and tore up the turf so badly that the Sox had to forfeit the nightcap. Years later, in 1993, Veeck helped build Minnesota's St. Paul Saints into the most successful independent minor league franchise in history with promotions his father would have been proud to call his own: haircuts during the ballgame for ten dollars and a mascot pig, "Saint Pig," that carried baseballs out to the home plate umpire.

Even before Veeck proved himself in St. Paul, he demonstrated a knack for the zany, as the following story told by John Kuhn illustrates. "I went to work for Veeck in 1990 when he was president of the Ft. Myers Miracle of the Florida State League," says Kuhn. "One day Veeck called me into his office and said he wanted me to become the Phantom of the Ballpark. This is a stunt that Veeck had used before to capitalize on the popularity of the Broadway play *The Phantom of the Opera* when he was with Pompano Beach. I wrote up a story about the Phantom of the Ballpark based on what Veeck told me, and we put it in the program. The Phantom supposedly was a Pompano Beach second baseman named Bix Bixby who had died in a collision with the center fielder and later had his ashes strewn about the old Pompano ballpark.

"The costume I put on for the part was homemade but quite elaborate. I wore a black Lone Ranger mask to hide my face, and over that I wore a catcher's mask, half of it painted white and half of it left black. I had a black 'Cheers of Ft. Lauderdale' sweatshirt that I turned inside out, and somewhere I found a black cape from an old Dracula Halloween costume. I'd also carry a black baseball bat with me and a finger flasher, which I got from a magic store. A finger flasher hooks over one of your fingers like a ring and has a button on it. And when you push the button, it shoots a miniature fireball of sparks.

"Now, normally, at some point during the game between innings we'd start playing *Phantom of the Opera* music, and I'd come out of the office where I dressed and into the stands to do my thing. Whenever the kids got close to me, they'd practically molest me, trying to pull off the costume to see who the

Phantom was. They kept getting bolder and bolder, so we decided to do something different. Veeck said, 'Can you bungee jump off the light tower?' He was serious, but there was no way I was going to do that, even if I hadn't been afraid of heights. So we decided that I would make a dramatic entrance by coming over the outfield wall.

"*The Phantom of the Opera* music was my cue, and when it started playing I climbed up on top of the left-field wall. The wall was about ten feet high, and once I got up there I got scared. I was holding the bat in one hand and trying to keep my balance with the other. There was a walkie-talkie in my pocket, and on it I could hear them calling me: 'Phantom, come in! Phantom, come in!' They didn't see me at first because they thought I was supposed to come over the right-field wall.

"In a little while the music stopped, and I knew that I had to do something, that I couldn't stay perched up on the wall forever. I didn't want to do it, but I jumped. I'd never broken a bone in my life, but I thought for sure this time I had broken my ankle. Worse, when I hit the ground, my thumb hit the button on the finger flasher, and the sparks flew and caught my cape on fire! I mean it started blazing! I rolled around on the ground to put the fire out, and then, in agony because of my ankle (which was not broken, although it sure felt broken) I started limping across the field. I looked like Lon Chaney dragging his club foot.

"Now, the kids got really excited, and they chased me all the way through the stands and up to the door of the club offices. I rushed through the doorway and then slammed the door behind me. I was leaning against the door, half burnt to a crisp, out of breath, the pain from my ankle almost causing me to pass out, and there was Veeck, standing in front of me. He started clapping, slowly, and then he said, 'Outstanding! Do it again tomorrow.'"

RUBE WADDELL

In addition to being a great pitcher, George Edward "Rube" Waddell, born October 13, 1876, was one of the greatest flakes in baseball history. Famous for possessing a deadly combination of a blazing fastball and a biting curve, the big lefty was even more notorious for the wacky stunts he pulled. Waddell often disappeared between starts to go fishing, drinking, or carousing, and he was known to have left the ballpark in the middle of a game more than once to chase after fire trucks, which held a special fascination for him. He also loved to lead parades, often left the diamond doing cartwheels after pitching his team to a win, and once took an off-season job wrestling alligators in Florida. Although Waddell's unpredictability and instability gave all his managers gray hair, the pious Connie Mack was able to handle Rube fairly well, and it was with Mack's Philadelphia A's that Waddell had his greatest successes in the major leagues: four consecutive 20-plus win seasons and 349 strikeouts in 1904, baseball's record until Sandy Koufax broke it sixty-one years later.

Waddell stories continue to emerge from the mists of the past; and the latest, about Rube's days with the Columbus Senators of the old Western League, is one that was discovered by baseball researcher Joe Santry. According to Santry, the Senators were going to start the season on the road, and all the players were assembled at the designated meeting place downtown. All but one. Rube Waddell was nowhere to be found. Cognizant of Waddell's idiosyncrasies, the players fanned out in a search of their star pitcher. The players eventually found Waddell, but not at a fire house, tavern, or house of ill repute. They found Waddell up a giant tree on the grounds of the state house, where he was trying to catch an albino squirrel that he wanted to take on the road as a team mascot!

WIFFLEMANIA!

Loved by every baseball fan between the ages of two and ninety-two, Wiffleball is the king of backyard bat and ball games. The game derives its name from the famous plastic baseball made in Shelton, Connecticut, which costs about a dollar. Like millions of American kids before and after him, Scott Peters fantasized about hitting a home run in the World Series while playing the game when he was growing up on the west side of Cincinnati. What Peters never dreamed was that as an adult he would become the founder of a Wiffleball tournament that has raised more than fifty thousand dollars for charity. Here's the story of how it happened.

When the thirty-six-year-old Peters was a young adult, he was casting about for something fun to do over the Labor Day weekend of 1991. Like a meatball right over the heart of the plate waiting to be creamed, the idea for a Wiffleball tournament wafted to him out of the memories of his happy childhood. He got together enough neighbors and old friends that he hadn't seen in a while to make four or five teams, and they played that first Wiffleball World Series—where else?—in his backyard, dressed up for the occasion with signs, banners, and bunting. And just like that, a tradition was born.

Unfortunately, the next June during Peters's wedding reception, his mother Mary Peters died of cancer. When Labor Day and the next Wiffleball World Series rolled around, there was only one thing to do: play the World Series in her honor and make the event a fund-raiser for a cancer charity by passing the hat and raffling off donated door prizes. Peters says that the idea was a natural because "The truest memory I have of my mother was of how much fun she had watching us play Wiffleball in our backyard."

Peters never made any attempt to promote the event, yet it quickly outgrew his backyard and its humble beginnings anyway. Some years ago the date was changed from Labor Day weekend to the middle of July, and Peters's wife Julie renamed the event Wifflemania! The 2003 tournament was played in a city park in Mason, Ohio, and it attracted forty-two teams and some five hundred players. Although most of the players hailed from the Cincinnati area, Wifflemania! 2003 drew players from thirteen states, including North Carolina, Florida, and Texas. Such is the lure of Wiffleball and the chance to help a good cause at the same time.

While other Wiffleball tournaments around the country might play by different rules, Wifflemania! goes by a set of rules and regulations that work for it. According to Peters, a middle school physical education teacher and an assistant football coach at Milford High School in Ohio, Wifflemania! is similar to co-ed softball. Each team must have a minimum of six players in the field, two of which must be female, but a team may bat as many different players as it wishes. Pitching is underhanded and slow; batters bat until they put the ball in play or strike out swinging, and the minimal umpiring duties are performed by players from teams not involved in the game at hand. The bases are thirty-five feet apart; leadoffs, stealing, sliding, and collisions are not allowed; and the home run distance is a uniform eighty-five feet. A typical game score is 15–5 or 2–1; "It depends," says Peters, "on which way the wind is blowing."

With their emphasis on fun and safety, the rules pretty much guarantee that players participate in Wifflemania! for the right reasons. There is no prize money at stake, and even the trophies won by the tournament champions and runners-up are comparatively modest: plaques with Polaroid team pictures mounted on them. Nevertheless, as Peters says, "The trophies might not sound like much, but when it comes down to the final few games, they play as if they're in the real World Series."

As much fun as Wifflemania! is, its higher purpose is what keeps Peters devoted to it, and the Opening Ceremonies, which emphasize the fight against cancer, are the most special part of the whole event for him and his family. In 2003, Peters, along with his dad, his sister, and his brother, finally made things official with the American Cancer Society by establishing the Mary Peters Memorial Fund. During the Opening Ceremonies in 2003 they set off fireworks and launched balloons, each of which had the name of a cancer attached to it. For 2004 Peters hopes to have a sky diver deliver the tournament's official first pitch Wiffleball. "Every year I try to one-up what we did the year before," says Peters. As for Mary Peters, her devoted son says, "For my family, Wifflemania! is a remembering day and a celebrating day. I know my mom is real proud of what we are doing with this tournament, just as she was always proud of us whenever we did something worthwhile. I know she's with us, for every pitch."

TED WILLIAMS

A serious beaning in Triple A limited his major league career to a single at-bat; but Bill Schlesinger, once a rising star in the Boston Red Sox organization, has many unforgettable baseball memories, several of which involve Ted Williams.

"The first time I met Ted," says Schlesinger, "he didn't say a thing to me. He only said something about me. In 1964 I played my first year of professional baseball, in Wellsville, New York, which was in the New York–Penn League. I was a very raw player, but I could do two things: I could run, and I could hit for power. I wound up leading the league in home runs that year with thirty-seven, which shocked the Red Sox, so toward the end of that summer Ted Williams and Bobby Doerr came over to Wellsville from New York City to check me out in person. The trip wasn't that big a deal for them because the Red Sox were in New York to play the Yankees. That morning I got in the batting cage to hit for them, and I was so nervous I could hardly stand up. I actually completely missed the first few pitches, and then about all I could do was hit foul balls or weak little grounders. Williams, Doerr, and my manager, Larry Thomas, were standing behind me, leaning on the cage, and Williams said to Larry, 'Are you sure you got the right kid here?' Doerr tried to calm me down, saying, 'Hey, kid, I know what you're going through. Take a few deep breaths and try to relax.' That helped me, and I started hitting the ball, but by then Ted had already walked away.

"The second time I saw Ted was the next year during the first week of spring training. He came up to me and said, 'So you're Schlesinger, huh?' I said I was.

"'Do you know who I am?' he asked. I said that I did.

"'Do you think I was a good hitter?' he asked.

"'I think you were a real good hitter,' I said.

"'Real good? I was the best goddamn hitter that ever lived!' he said. 'And don't you forget it.'

"After Ted got that off his chest, he told me that he liked my swing, that he thought I had a chance to make it as a big leaguer. And I've never forgotten that, either."

"Ted loved to talk about hitting," says Schlesinger, "and he was always ready to do so, but never in front of pitchers. He hated pitchers, even our own pitchers. Plus, he thought pitchers were stupid, so he wouldn't talk if there were any pitchers in the clubhouse.

"Ted hated sportswriters even more than he hated pitchers, because he thought that they never got their stories straight. 'They always screw things up. They're known for that,' he'd say.

"Anyway, one day there was nobody in the clubhouse but Ted and five or six of us hitters, and Ted was giving us a lesson in hitting, telling us all about his theories and philosophy. Ten minutes into this discussion, five sportswriters came into the clubhouse, walking single file, one after the other. Ted immediately stopped talking to us and said, 'Who the hell are you guys?'

"The first guy said, 'I'm so-and-so with the *Orlando Sentinel*,' and the next guy started to say, 'I'm so-and-so with the *Miami Herald*,' but before he could get it out Ted interrupted him. 'No sportswriters in the clubhouse while I'm talking about hitting,' he said. 'Get out. I don't want you in here.'

"And those guys turned around without stopping or even slowing down and walked right out of the clubhouse, still in single file. They didn't miss a beat, nor did they dare question Ted's authority to kick them out."

"Ted had been retired for five years when I went to my first spring training with the Red Sox," says Schlesinger, "but he could still swing the bat. He wasn't just a big talker. I saw him take batting practice one day, and he was amazing. He told the pitcher, 'Just try to throw the ball over the plate.' He hit nine straight rockets, either off the wall or over it, the first three to right field, the second three to center, and the last three to left. It was just an amazing display of power and place hitting, because normally Ted was strictly a pull hitter. He pulled everything to the right.

"Another thing I'll never forget: Both Ted and Bobby Doerr had fungo bats that spring. Fungo bats are real long and skinny bats that coaches use to hit practice grounders and fly balls, and coaches usually tape up the barrels of fungo bats with white trainer's tape to keep the barrels from splintering. Well, toward the end of spring training, after Ted and Doerr had been using their fungo bats for weeks, we were standing around the batting cage. Ted said, 'Hey, Bobby, look at this. I want to show you something. Let me see your fungo bat.'

"Doerr handed his bat to Ted, and when Ted held it up you could see that the tape on his bat, which was about a foot and a half in length around the bat, was dirty all over from the smudges made when the bat hit the ball. Ted then held up his bat for comparison, and it was completely different. There was a ring around his bat where the sweet spot would be that was almost black, and it was only about two inches wide, which meant that Ted had been hitting the ball with the same exact part of the bat all spring. He looked at Doerr with a big grin on his face and said, 'Bobby, that's the difference between a .400 hitter and a .200 hitter.'"

"My final Ted Williams story revolves around Ted's belief that you always set yourself for the fastball and adjust to the curve, not vice versa," says Schlesinger, "because the fastball is just too fast to adjust to. Ted preached this constantly, and all of us in the Red Sox organization believed that we were fastball hitters.

"I started the season with the Red Sox in 1965, not because I was ready to play in the big leagues—I wasn't—but because of a rule that no longer exists. At the time, if another team offered you a contract in a higher league than the one you were playing in, they could claim you. The Red Sox didn't know what to do with me, but they were afraid of losing me if they kept me in the minors, so they took me north with them to start the season. I just sat on the bench and watched.

"We started out in Detroit, and Ted, who usually left the team after spring training, stayed on for a while for some reason. We were facing Denny McLain that day, and before the game Ted told Tony Conigliaro, whom he really liked, to look for McLain's fastball. Tony's first time at bat McLain, who had a great fastball, threw him nothing but curves and changeups, and Tony, who was in his second year in the majors, struck out. 'Don't worry about it, Tony, keep looking fastball,' said Ted.

"Next time up it was the same thing. Nothing but breaking and off-speed pitches, and Tony struck out again. 'I'm telling ya, look fastball,' said Ted.

"Third time up, McLain threw Tony more junk. He wouldn't even throw him a fastball as a waste pitch, and Tony struck out again. By this time Tony was so frustrated he was almost crying. 'I can't hit that crap he's throwing me,' said Tony.

" 'Don't worry about it,' said Ted. 'Just keep looking fastball.'

" 'I am, but he's never going to throw me one,' said Tony.

" 'Just do what I tell you, Tony,' Ted continued to insist.

"McLain was pitching a great game, and by the time Tony came up for the fourth time, it was the top of the ninth, and the Tigers were ahead 1–0. Three more outs and the game was over. McLain got the first two guys out, and then Rico Petrocelli, hitting in front of Tony, hit a two-hopper to short. That should have been it, but the shortstop bobbled the ball and threw too late to get Rico at first. Tony came up again, and McLain pitched him the same way he had all day. McLain ran the count even at 2-2, and then he finally threw a fastball, the first one he'd thrown to Tony all day, and Tony was waiting for it. He hit the ball so hard it struck the facing of the roof in left field for a two-run homer and bounced all the way back to the shortstop, who picked it up in shallow left field. Ted was just thrilled. 'See! What'd I tell you?' he said to Tony. The Tigers went down one-two-three in the bottom of the ninth, and we won the game 2–1. Afterward in the locker room Ted was still excited about it, and he said something like, 'Tony had to hit it, but I should get half the credit for that home run!' "

WORLD'S GREATEST BATTING COACH

Howard Carrier, of Fairfield, Ohio, is a man of great girth and even greater faith. He is also the world's greatest batting coach. Here is his story.

Howard and his wife, Susan, have one child, a son named Kenny who was born in 1983. When Kenny was seven years old, he jumped on a friend's bicycle and began riding down the street. Unknown to Kenny, the bike had no brakes, because the father of the boy the bike belonged to had stripped the bike of its brakes in order to put them on a different bike. Unable to stop the bike, Kenny flew the length of his friend's driveway, bounded down a steep embankment behind the house, and hurtled into a tree the circumference of a light pole. The accident crushed the right side of Kenny's skull and caused three brain contusions.

Kenny was rushed to the hospital, where doctors, and his father, fought desperately to save his life. Kenny was first taken to Christ Hospital, where he began having seizures. The doctors there asked Howard for permission to remove the top of Kenny's skull, a procedure Howard felt was extremely risky. As a doctor knelt on top of Kenny's chest and struggled to insert tubes down the unconscious boy's throat, a nurse came over to Howard and whispered to him, "Get your son out of here, or he's going to die. He needs to be at Children's Hospital."

Howard told the doctors he wanted Kenny moved to Children's. They ignored him. He pleaded with them, to no avail, so then he demanded that his son be moved. A security guard came over and confronted Howard, who told the guard, "That's my son they're working on. If you don't get out of my way, I'm going to grab your throat and rip it out." A doctor intervened, telling Howard, "If we move Kenny to Children's, he'll die. He'll never make it. Besides, there's not an air-care helicopter available right now to move him, even if we wanted to."

"I'll drive him in my car," said Howard, who remained steadfast in his desire to transfer Kenny. A short time later a helicopter became available, and the doctors finally relented and allowed Kenny to be transferred to Children's Hospital. There, doctors put the boy into a narcotic-induced coma to control the seizures. They also drilled a hole into his skull into which they inserted a wire to measure inner cranial pressure. Kenny stabilized but was still in considerable danger, as it was a constant battle to keep the pressure in his brain down. Howard and his wife prayed constantly that Kenny's life might be spared, and they took turns staying at his bedside around the clock. At one point Kenny started having trouble breathing, and no one noticed it except Howard, who could tell that something was wrong by a change in the color of a birthmark on Kenny's face. Howard alerted the nurses, and when the doctor did an X-ray on Kenny's chest he discovered that the breathing tube had slipped out of place, allowing only one lung to function properly. A couple of days later, after Kenny came out of the coma, his veins began to collapse. No one could find a vein to give him the medicine he desperately needed, and the nurse and the doctor left the room in panic. Kenny asked, "Dad, am I gonna die?"

"No," said Howard. "If God had wanted you, he'd have taken you two days ago." Even though the tubes that had been down Kenny's throat for a week made swallowing extremely painful, Howard convinced him to take the medicine orally, and another crisis was averted. Kenny stayed a total of two weeks in the hospital, and while he was there the Carriers saw many kids who didn't make it. "I was so happy when Kenny was able to leave," said Howard, "because while we were there, it was nothing but death, death, death."

Although he suffered a little paralysis, Kenny made a remarkable recovery and soon began playing T-ball. As Kenny got older and more serious about the game, Howard wanted to give his son every advantage. On the advice of a friend whose son played with Kenny on a summer team, Howard sent Kenny to a batting instructor for private lessons. Howard could not have been more disappointed. The so-called expert charged a lot of money for his services, yet Kenny didn't improve at all. Worse, Howard suspected that the instructor couldn't teach Kenny how to hit because he really didn't have the knowledge to do so.

This was the point when Howard decided to take things into his own hands. He decided to become his own batting instructor. Carrier read every book on hitting he could find. He studied the theories of Dusty Baker, Charlie Lau, Mike Schmidt, Ted Williams, and others, and he found something useful in almost all of them. When Howard was satisfied that he understood the science of hitting, he combined his knowledge with a teaching philosophy based on that of W. Edwards Demming, who taught that to effect continuous improvement one has to "operationally define it [the thing being taught] in measurable and observable terms that reasonable people can agree on."

Howard put a batting cage in his backyard, turned his garage into a baseball batting laboratory, and invented a number of ingenious devices and instructional gadgets to help him get his message across. He began coaching hitting, using his son Kenny and his friends as his test subjects, and the results were dramatic improvements in their abilities to hit a baseball. Noticing the improvement, the dads of other kids on Kenny's summer team wanted to know who was teaching Kenny. "When I told them that I was the one who was coaching Kenny, they couldn't believe it," says Howard. Their incredulity was understandable, as Howard had never played an inning of baseball on any level, not even Little League, in his life. Not only that but, at 535 pounds, he had a most unathletic physique.

Nevertheless, Howard Carrier proved the old adage that hitting a baseball is mostly mental. More important, he approached coaching with the idea that "if you treat children like they are snowflakes, knowing that they are all unique, they will amaze you with their hidden talents!"

Word of the great improvement of Kenny Carrier and his buddies spread quickly, and soon parents around Cincinnati were sending their youngsters to Howard for personal batting instruction. More than four hundred aspiring young sluggers have been tutored at the Carrier home, and Howard has never accepted a dime for his services; although grateful parents insist that he accept token gifts, such as soda pop and bottled water, which he usually winds up redistributing to the kids. There can be no arguing with the effectiveness of Carrier's methods. According to the local newspapers, his students are among the area high school batting leaders every spring, and Kenny earned a baseball scholarship to the College of Charleston in South Carolina. Even ex–major league ballplayers who now coach kids' teams come to Howard to learn how to teach what they were able to do in the major leagues. As for Howard, who retired after a twenty-three-year career at General Electric, he is happy being a full-time batting coach and the servant of others. Uninterested in making money or in feeding his ego, he continues his work joyfully, "as a thank-you to God."

INDEX